The **Naked** Jesus: [Dedication Page]

I would like to pass my love to Shellene for being there through all the hard times and good times. No man could wish for a better friend, partner, companion, or love – You are an amazing person who is open, honest, and direct. Without you in my life, this book would have never jumped from my brain to paper.

To Heather, Steve, Julian and Em – our family – you brighten my day. All of you are a blessing in my life.

To Caedmon Michael who is not only my Editor but my friend and second voice. Caedmon's ability to know what I am thinking when he reads my stuff is amazing. He is able to read and help me give voice to my thoughts.

The Naked Jesus: [What Others Are Saying]

John O'Keefe takes his faith seriously; but it's not the kind of faith that popular Christianity generally understands. He's in pursuit of the kind of faith that renders the Naked Jesus of the Gospels intelligible to an often self-absorbed world. With a distinctive voice, John O'Keefe challenges the listless believe-ism that has come to characterize Christianity in America, opting instead for a robust version of faith that asks of followers to love the Naked Jesus even more than their own lives.

Derek Penwell is Lecturer in Theology at Bellarmine University,Senior Minister at Douglass Blvd Christian Church and Lecturer in Humanities at University of Louisville)

John O'Keefe's quirky, candid wisdom offers a lifeline to people who are "drowning in the shallow end" of organized religion, inviting readers to dive into an ocean of freedom and grace.

*Sarah Thebarge
Author of "The Invisible Girls"*

In The Naked Jesus, John O'Keefe takes off the gloves and transparently identifies the institutional church as his ideological opponent, exposing their inconsistencies, hypocrisies and misuse of what he calls the "collective narrative" (a.k.a. the bible). His perspective of Jesus leadership and life is more street theologian than teaching pastor. Although his passion for Jesus is unassailable it's doubtful that he will be receiving many invitations to speak in church given his penchant for admitting to such heresies as being a liberal who not only accepts but *wants* gay people in the community of faith. Be that as it may, be careful about ignoring O'Keefe because as William Gibson (the inventor of the term cyberspace) is famously quoted as saying "the future is already here, it's just not evenly distributed yet". O'Keefe's Naked

Jesus is a peek into the future that many followers of Jesus currently enjoy and are actively working to make the new normal."

Jim Henderson
Provocateur, Producer and Author
Jim and Casper Go To Church

John O'Keefe strips the cultural-clothing we have added to Christ in The Naked Jesus. John asks us to rip off our own clothing- baggage and context given stuff- so we can see the Naked Jesus. I hope this work can help many who gave up their fundamentalistic faith to know they can still be Christians.

Bec Cranford-Smith
Community Activist
Co-Founder of "The Church of The Misfits"

John O'Keefe helps us, in plain language, understand how and why institutional religion has failed — and is failing - to capture so many hearts and imaginations of followers of Jesus in today's world. Eschewing "feel good" superficial religiosity for a richer, more in-depth exploration of the naked vulnerability of the Christian gospel, he strips away the jargon and ivory tower mentality of an aging church, exposing us anew to that which was so compelling about the life and teaching of Jesus to begin with.

Christian Piatt, author of Blood Doctrine and postChristian
www.christianpiatt.com

The only thing "naked" about this book is John's willingness to be vulnerable. He has stripped down to his emotional and spiritual birthday-suit in an effort to simply be real. The value in that is how it leads to a path of actually following Jesus rather than following the institution that claims to point to him. If you question the Church and its dogma, I suspect you'll value John's journey.

Mark Sandlin
Co-Host at The Moonshine Jesus Show
Owner/Blogger at The God Article
Ordained Minister at Vandalia Presbyterian Church

There is a third view, and that is "what the church could be", or more importantly "what we could be" and that is exactly where The Naked Jesus fits. John's revelation (too good to pass up) of his passage into and out of conservative mainstream Christianity is a journey too many of us have undertaken, and many have yet to undertake, unfortunately. What he offers is not a condemnation of the church, he instead offers a vision of hope, a vision that if embarked upon will hurt, and will change us, for the better. He shows us the choice we can make, if we have the courage to do so.

Peter Lambert
Sometime Pastor/Theologian & Thug for God
Lowbrowtheology.com

An open conversation:
What Do You Think? After reading *The Naked Jesus* let's have a conversation: johncasimirokeefe@gmail.com

OR

Join the conversation on Social Media:
facebook.com/johncasimirokeefe (Author's Page)
facebook.com/pages/The-Naked-Jesus (Book's Page)
Post a review on Amazon.com (good or bad)

The **Naked** Jesus; A Journey Out of Christianity and Into Christ

CHAPTER ZERO:
[The Preface]

 There comes a time in everyone's life where they question the presumptions they've lived under for years. I'm not talking about finding out there's no Santa Claus, Tooth Fairy, or Easter Bunny – though I can assure you when I was 17 years old and found out they were not real, it freaked me out.

> **THE LESS YOU TALK. THE MORE YOU'RE LISTENED TO.**
>
> *Pauline Phillips*

I'm talking about something bigger, something brighter.

That time came for me in the late 90's when I decided I would no longer call myself a *Christian*.

I remember it clearly, I posted on a ginkworld.net[1] message board (back when they were all the rage), and all hell broke loose. I had just finished writing, and posting, an article entitled "*95 Postmodern Thesis,*"[2] a kind of rant about the state of the current church modeled, feeding off of Martin Luther. When I posted my statement on the board, people were angry and confused, and they tried to pressure me to change my mind. To be honest, I waffled for a few years before I held fast to my decision. I am not sure who said it first, but I learned that *if I could no longer accept the things I couldn't change, it was time to change the things I couldn't accept* – for me, that was self-identifying as a "*Christian.*"

---

[1] I founded ginkworld.net back in the early 90's to be a voice for the than "postmodern Christians" looking to express themselves about the current state of the church.
[2] http://ginkworld.net/2009/08/95-postmodern-thesis/

At the time, the current face of the church was something I could not accept; and to be honest with you, very little has changed.

I didn't deny the label *Christian* because I couldn't or didn't want to follow the teachings of Jesus, but because I *did* want to follow those teachings. I wanted my life to change so I could live the teachings of the Naked Jesus,[3] a Jesus stripped of the brand identity of the Jesus®[4] (the Institutional Church[5]) proclaimed by the brand holders. I realized I wasn't called to be like other Christians, I was invited to be more like Christ.

---

[3] The Naked Jesus is the Jesus we see without all the human trappings. The Naked Jesus is the Jesus I desire to follow, not the man-made Jesus of the Institutional Church.

[4] Jesus® is the trademark of the Institutional Church, and no permission was given for the use of the term.

[5] I will share a definition of the Institutional Church in a later chapter. The reason for this is because I desire you to think about that term, struggle with the term and come to grips with your personal definition before I share mine. Keep in mind, a "institutional church" does not have to be a denomination.

As I saw it, and still see it, much of what some call *Christianity* was centered more on the institutional church's teachings on the branded Jesus® and less on the teachings of the words of the Naked Jesus. So, I rejected the label *Christian* and started calling myself a *Follower of the Teachings of Jesus.*[6] At that moment, I realized I had to journey out of the institutional church[7] and into the arms of the Naked Jesus.

This book is a process of that journey, not complete by any stretch of the imagination because my life and faith are always in process; I'm always growing and willing to hear the voices of others. I'm continually wrestling with what I hear the Naked Jesus saying and what I hear the institutional church saying, desiring to follow the teachings of the Naked Jesus, not those of the institutional church.

---

[6] Sometimes I used the term *Follower of Jesus*, or *Follower of the Way.*
[7] The term "institutional church" does not mean oldline, or mainline denominstions – it can be assigned to a non-denominational church also.

I've been a coward in that struggle. Inside, I have contemplated the Naked Jesus while continuing to toe the company line of the institutional church on the outside in order to keep me safe. That didn't always work out for me; I slipped and had to cover my tracks more than once. Yes, I define that as being a coward.

I feared losing my friends, my ministry, my status, and my job. I hid behind the company line to maintain my safety and fund this silly habit of eating I developed as a youth. I feared what others would think of me, what others would say about me, and how they would push me aside. I feared sharing my inner thoughts, my inner conflicts, because I knew, I just knew, people would push me aside and call me stupid. How did I know that would happen? Because I saw it happen to others with more courage than I had. However, the more I read, the more I prayed, and the more I thought about what the Naked Jesus had to say and how so many seemed to twist that to fit their political agenda, personal need or protect some crazy notion of the institutional church, the more I felt I needed to grow a pair, share where my heart was, and let the chips fall where they may.

Some may see this book as confronting, or even angry at some points, but my goal is neither. I have no desire to confront and I am not angry. My prayer is that you see this book as a starting point and find your voice to stand against the Jesus® you are expected to believe in and learn instead to follow the Naked Jesus.

Over time I grew a pair – I hope they are big enough to share everything in my heart and journey.

SECTION I
[The back story]

Every character has a backstory. If you have ever acted, the first question you asked about your character would have been, "*What's the character's backstory?*" Why, because knowing the backstory helps you play the character with integrity, with emotion, and with direction. You understand how and why your character responds in certain situations and how your character will interact with others characters in the play.

This section of *The Naked Jesus* tells my backstory. I will share a bit of myself and my faith journey, but more importantly, I will ask questions and invite you to think about possible answers. My interest is not in the answers you come up with, but in the development of more –deeper – questions.

CHAPTER ONE:
[Why This Book?]

 As part of my backstory, I need to share with you the reason I wrote this book; why this book is so important to me and why I would love for everyone to read it: *When we find the Naked Jesus, we uncover the freedom to put our faith into action*; we desire to *do* something and not just *believe* something; we stop talking

IF YOU CAN T FEED A HUNDRED PEOPLE. THEN FEED JUST ONE.
Mother Teresa

a good game and get dirty playing the game; we are freed from the institutional church structure that desires to define us and stand invited to the table where the Naked Jesus help us discover who we are; we are freed from the garbage it brings to the party; and we no longer swim in the slime of the shallow end of the pool. My desire is to help you find the

Naked Jesus who says *"First things first. Your business is life, not death. Follow me. Pursue life."*[8] I so want to pursue life; I want *you* to pursue life. You see, for me, what I have found in my faith journey is that the Jesus® we are introduced to in the institutional church is so confined, so small, so one-sided, so monocultural, that living in the mystery of the Naked Jesus is lost to the rules, regulations and requirements of following a belief system (religion). When we follow Jesus® we are living in the business of life – following the Naked Jesus, we pursue life.

Before I go further, let me say this: I don't think people *need* to leave the church[9] to find the Naked Jesus. You don't. All you need to do is realize that you are to pursue life, a life

---

[8] Matthew 8:22

[9] Notice I did not say you should stay in an institutional church – those you should leave. I have found in my journey of faith that the Disciples of Christ and the United Church of Christ are two of the best churches out there.

where following *supersedes* believing[10] at the core of your

faith. By sticking around we might be able to help the

institutional church transition into an active, open, missional

and accepting *Community of Faith*.[11] But, if this is impossible,

if you find yourself abused and confronted by the institutional

gatekeepers because you are asking questions, you think

differently, you want action instead of talk, find a Community

of Faith where you can ask your questions in safety and where

they are doing something with their faith, not just writing

checks so others can do the dirty work – or what I like to think

of as the fun shit we should be doing – for them. In living out

---

[10] I realize that there are some who will see this statement as the
pendulum swing the other way – that there needs to be balance between
believing and action, and you may be right – but read on and see where
I'm going.
[11] A Community of Faith is a place where people can ask any questions and
do not get the corporate answer. It is a safe place that welcomes everyone,
regardless. It is a place that desires to follow and not just believe.

our faith in community, in common unity (*Koinonia*[12]), it is important that we understand we are co-participants, co-creators, in developing a community of faith; deeper than that, we are co-creators in bring to life the Kingdom of the Divine around us – no one can take that away from our being.

One more thing – and this is rather important – I am not searching for the *Historical Anything*. I'll leave that to the history nerds (*I'm a theological nerd*). In my twisted little mind, when I think in terms of finding the *Historical* Jesus, or the *Historical* Christ, or the *Historical* Church, or *Historical* Christianity, or the *Historical anything*, all I find are boring facts filled with historical figures I can't relate to, located in

---

[12] According to Wikipedia, "*Koinonia* is a transliterated form of the Greek word, κοινωνία, which means communion, joint participation; the share which one has in anything, participation, a gift jointly contributed, a collection, a contribution, etc. It identifies the idealized state of fellowship and unity that should exist within the Christian church, the Body of Christ" http://en.wikipedia.org/wiki/Koinonia. We will be talking more about Koinonia in Chapter Nine.

places with names I can't pronounce and locations I will never

visit or connect with in any way.[13] Besides, no matter how

hard you or I try, *we* can never fully understand what it was

like to live in the first centuries; heck, it is almost impossible

for to grasp the mindset of the last century. That is not to say

that history is not important. It is. History can help put things

in perspective. But trying to place things into a historical

context always brings about debate on whether the Naked

Jesus was a *real* historical figure or if the words shared in the

collective narrative were the *real* words of the Naked Jesus. I

have no problem with the Naked Jesus as a real person,

walking the earth and teaching us how we can connect with

the Divine; I have no issues accepting the words recorded in

---

[13] I always love hearing about pastors taking people on trips to the Holy Land (sense the sarcasm). For me, it is the realization that if you can get 10 people to go on the trip the pastor's expenses are covered by the company. Also, most people in the church can't afford such a trip – so only the "well to do" get to go.

collective narrative as the words of this Naked Jesus.[14] I am not interested in playing the '*did Jesus really say that*' game. When we play the historical game, we soon find we are playing the '*pick and choose*' game, which always seems to fit into the corporate game.

I started this book about ten months ago and scrapped it. Why? Because I was trying to write something things too linear – I tried to place ideas and emotions neatly into categories; packaging them into nice little packages with pretty blue bows (and I suck at that) – and linear never brings about emotional or spiritual comfort. I knew better, but I was following the lead and advice of others who told me that that was the *best way* of writing this book. I surrendered my freedom for the will of others and it didn't work.

---

[14] I also have no issue with some of the writings left out of the "official bible."

As my backstory developed, I rejected the corporate game, this book started to take shape. I soon found myself thinking differently, yet always focused on the Naked Jesus. But it never seemed to fail, those who desire everyone toe the company line soon got involved.

Every time I started a chapter, I got pissed-off. I found myself forcing words out of my mind and following some misguided systematic theology that is just not me. Each time, I tried to hold back *my* thoughts for the thoughts of *others* and it drove me crazy (*not quite bat-shit crazy*). I was told to leave certain things out because it could *hurt* others or cause them to think *poorly* of me. I was told that certain theological conclusions I came to were not supported by the institution, and they should be changed. I was told to watch my language as to not alienate some readers. I was told to ask myself one important question as I wrote: "*Will what I write sell books?*" That's not a good place for my head.

Do I want to sell books? *Sure*, I would love it is everyone read this book. That's why writers write books; we want people to read our books and share them with others so we can eat (*that monkey is still on my back*) and pay our bills. This is my fourth book, and I can assure you I am not even close to being middleclass. But selling books isn't – or shouldn't be – the reason anyone writes; it's not why I write. The reason to write is to get the information out of your head and heart and into the head heart of others. Writing based only on sales is a pretty shitty way to write something that comes from your heart and soul, especially writing books on theology which will never make you rich.[15] My friends, and a few Mentors, didn't want me to write anything others might use to label me a *heretic*. All I could think was, *too late, that ship has already sailed.*

What got me the most during this process were all the decisions others were making about this book (*including cover design*) that had nothing to do with what I wanted to say, with what my heart was exploding to expose. Their input had nothing to do with me or what I was writing. In one conversation with a Publisher, it was suggested that I change the title of the book to something *sellable*. Soon, I realized I was writing *their book*, not the one kicking around in my head. I was trying to make others happy and found myself forcing my thoughts to go their direction; I was not comfortable with

---

[15] My friend Leonard Sweet told me once that when I write a book on theology, call it a book about *Leadership*, because books on Leadership sell better than books on theology – *Hope you like my new book on Leadership*

that direction. I was selling out my views and beliefs under some twisted idea of not wanting to alienate or offend the institutional church so I could sell books. I found myself writing in the negative. My heart was just not in it. It felt more *forced* than *flowing*. While I always look forward to writing, I found myself pushing this book aside. I soon realized I was surrendering my voice for the voice of the institution; *just when I thought I was out, they pulled me back in again*.

My heart kept telling me I was writing for the needs of the institution, not to share the amazing collective narrative of hope found in the Naked Jesus.

So I did the only thing I could do.

I trashed the first copy.

After completely erasing the first version of this book from my head, my heart, my hard drive, and the cloud, this second incarnation took shape. Because it's coming from my heart — the place my writing needs to start — it will not be *linear* in any way, shape, or form. Linear thought confuses me because it doesn't allow for all the different ways things are connected. Life and theology are far less a string held tight, and far more a *ball of string* where things overlap and connect at different points.[16] I needed to be honest with myself and with others. I needed to express my thoughts as they came to me — how I think of them, how they move me, how they excite me, and how they enlighten me — no matter how twisted the ball of string may get.

---

[16] What I love about this *ball of string* imagery is that in any ball of sting there are knots, some you can untie and others you have to let go.

I hold no hard feeling towards those who wished I traveled in another direction. I know they meant well.

Granted, *starting over* totally screwed-up all the deadlines I was working under,[17] killed far too many trees for my tastes, and I spent a small fortune in ink, but this is where I need to be. Will it sell? Who knows, that's up to you. All I know is that it is out of my head – and now there is room for other things to take root.

I need to speak to the words the Divine is leading me to speak. This book is birthed from my heart, not from the depths of book sales, editors' desires, the publisher's needs, or anything else – it is simply me sharing with you what is in my heart and how the Naked Jesus moved me from the *prison* of

---

[17] My original plan was to have this book out by Easter, 2014.

Christianity[18] to the *freedom* of being a Follower of the Naked Jesus; it is birthed out of a desire to move past the institutional church.

In this book, I will share with you my search for the Naked Jesus and what I found. I will be honest with you in my faith journey because I have found in the past that when I write from the heart – in my own voice and not from the voice of others (*no matter how meaningful they are*) – people write and tell me how my writing has helped them: helped them find their voice; helped them make a stance; helped them find their faith and move them forward on their faith journey. I believe there are a great many people like me searching for something deeper, something life changing, something

---

[18] *Prison of Christianity* may sound harsh, but when freedom is removed from your faith journey, *prison* is the only word that fits.

meaningful, and I believe the Naked Jesus is the beginning of that search.

I know there are a great many people who have zero interest in the institutional church, zero interest in the company line, zero interest in speaking *Christianese*, zero interest in the crap fed to us by those who use Jesus® as a weapon or political tool. If you're like me, if you want to move past all the crap placed on Jesus®, then you will want to toss out the *American Jesus*, the *Magic Jesus*, and the *Political Jesus*. And, if in the process the baby gets tossed out with the bath water, so be it; this is why there is a Resurrection. Many of us do not desire to see Jesus® as the Naked Jesus: we desire to see the Naked Jesus; to hear his words, to live his teachings, no matter how challenging they may be; to know a Naked Jesus who stands on his own, without all the trappings we place upon him; to see a Naked Jesus who leads us to say '*I desire to be like him.*' This is not the Jesus® the institutional church shares with us, but it is one I desire to follow. While I stated this in Chapter Zero, it is important enough to say again: *I have no desire to act like a Christian; I have been invited to act like Christ.*

As I started the process of moving past the abuse, power struggles and the blind demands of the institutional church I started the process of moving past all the hype and garbage of the institutional church's Jesus® placed upon me; to do that, I needed to ask myself some questions:

Who is the Jesus® the church was selling?
Can I refuse that Jesus® and go in search of the Naked Jesus?
What is the difference between Jesus® and the Naked Jesus? What, if anything, is the same?
Can I move past the sales force that insists I buy their understanding of Jesus®?

Most importantly, am I willing to be changed in the process?

I want the Naked Jesus who loves me for me and invites me to love others, for who they are, not who I demand them to be. As I open my heart and share with you my inner thoughts, my inner search, I pray you will see the Naked Jesus I have come to know and love. But before you see the Naked Jesus, a little preparation is needed.

CHAPTER TWO:
[A Bit of My Back Story]

 To start off, let me address something you may be thinking: '*How can any Pastor write a book about their journey OUT of Christianity?*' Well, it's easy – I guess I'm just that kind of guy.

I could never figure out why the Divine wanted me to be a Pastor in the first place. I mean, think about it: I suck at the institutional

THE PURPOSE OF A STORYTELLER IS NOT TO TELL YOU HOW TO THINK, BUT TO GIVE YOU QUESTIONS TO THINK UPON.
— Brandon Sanderson, *The Way of Kings*

church, I'm not a very good representative of the brand, I don't look-like or act-like other pastors, and even though others in the institutional church have told me to change my appearance (*on a regular basis*), I have no desire to do so. I mean really, look at me: I have no problem questioning

authority; I'm perfectly comfortable sitting in a local bar,

buying a pitcher of beer (*local micro-brew*), setting up four

empty glasses on a table with a sign that reads, "*Join Me,*

Let's Talk Theology;" I shave my head;[19] have plugs in my

ears,[20] a long goatee, and tats; and I've been known to smoke

a good cigar and on occasion add a shot of whiskey to that

beer. Why would the Divine ever think I would make a good

pastor? I don't even own a pair of khaki pants or a powder

blue leisure suit. I have been amazed at the churches who tell

me, '*We would love to have you as our Pastor, but...*' and you

can finish that sentence any way you desire.[21]

---

[19] The Divine took half my hair, so I figured I would shave off the other half.

[20] Zero gauge ear piercings

[21] I had one church tell me that they were uncomfortable with the idea of making me their new pastor because they felt I was going to "make" them get out of the church and into the community – and they did not like that idea.

While I'm cool with most parts of a *good* liturgy (*ones that explore the mystery of the Divine*), I think most hymns suck (*amazingly poor theology*). I love the candles, but find most of the contemporary stuff boring, out of touch, and a bit pretentious – fog machines; I mean really, a fog machine?

No, I just can't figure it out. I sometimes think the Divine wanted to place me in my own personal *Kobayashi Maru*,[22] and laugh as I struggled to figure out a solution – but here I am, a Pastor. The Divine must know something I don't.

As I've shared in my earlier books,[23] I was not raised in the church. For a long time I thought that was a bad thing, but now I see it as a good thing. Not being raised in the church means I don't carry the invisible monster of dysfunction and

---

[22] That's a no-win scenario, for you non-Trekkers.
[23] There is a list at the back of this book – just in case you want to help me pay off my student loans and feed my family.

abuse those raised in the church have the misfortune of carrying.[24] While not being raised in the church has its own pitfalls, I have seen those raised in the church weighed down under a butt load of meaningless crap, some so burdened they can hardly stand under the weight of a load they believe important to their journey, but isn't. I admit that sounds rather argumentative, but if you were raised in the church you know what I am talking about.

Soon after I made the decision to *believe* in the Jesus® others told me about, I was convinced by those who "*brought me to Jesus®*" that the only real place one could go to learn about that Jesus® was *The Church*. Oh yeah, I fell into the *you can't be a Christian if your don't go to church* trap. It was just a matter of time before I found myself in the middle of all the

---

[24] I will admit that when I hear my friends share stories about their *Christian Camp* experiences I am always a bit bummed; if I had gone to Christian Camp I would have lost my virginity at a much earlier age.

garbage we call *The Church,* being weighted down, gasping for air.

When we lived in California we had an amazing swimming pool.[25] If I could share one bit on knowledge about pool ownership it would be this, pools are a great way to waste your time and all your money just trying to keep the darn thing clean. Soon we found we could hardly control the slime that formed at the bottom of the shallow end of the pool. Our *Pool Guy* told us that shallow ends of pools were always a bit slimier because it was easier for the slime to grow; it seems that the shallow end offered a better environment for slime to take hold. Our Pool Guy tried to explain to me how this happened, but it didn't register in my mind – chemistry was never my strong suit; he said it had something to do with the

---

[25] When we brought Danu, our Irish Wolfhound/Great Dane mix, home for the first time and took her off the leash, she ran out the back door and landed in the pool. We could never get her to go into the pool again.

sun, the Ph balance and the depth of the water (but all I heard was, "*Blah, blah, blah, blah, blah*"). He told us we had two options. We could either add a butt load of chemicals at a massive hit to the wallet, or drain the pool and fill it with fresh water. Either way, the wallet was going to get a big hit.

One day, while adding a small fortune in chemicals to the pool, it hit me: *This is the Church*. The Institutional Church is the shallow end of the pool. We spend so much time and money trying to keep the slim down, but it never works. For me, it was time to drain the pool.

Soon after joining the Institutional church, I found myself swimming in the shallow end of all the misguided traditions others claim to be *Christianity* and didn't like what I found; swimming in the shallow end means you swim with a great deal of slime – which makes you feel gross. Most of those traditions have lost their meaning, and those who still desire everyone follow them have lost the ability to explain them — they just refuse change (*got to keep the slime growing*).

After joining an institutional church, my eyes were opened wide to a place filled with silly rules, blind traditions, abusive systems and people who cared more about themselves, the programs, the color of the carpet, the flowers on Holy Days, or the building, and less about helping others; when I was serving a Downtown Church, one of the Leaders asked me, "*It might be right to minister to the poor, but do we have to do it in our building?*" The institutional church sees the community as a pool of prospects, not a place for service.

I soon found it to be a place with heavy, draining, meaningless, strained traditions, where the structure supported the institution[26] and was out of tune with the world I lived in; a place where I believed the teachings of the Naked Jesus were camouflaged by the trappings of the American culture and the Political Right, and the Jesus® that made them comfortable; to me it seemed to be a perfect environment for the slime to grow.

I struggled to balance the identity of the Naked Jesus from my reading of the *Collective Narrative*[27] and the Jesus® the institutional church tried to shove down my throat (*and I do mean shove*). No matter how hard I tried, I couldn't connect the two; the dots were just not there.

---

[26] When I served in the UMC, our District Superintendent refused to remove names off our membership role (even people who passed away three years ago) because it would affect the amount of money we gave in to the institution.

[27] I am sure you have been wondering what I mean by "the collective narrative?" I call Scripture "the collective narrative" because I see it as a collection of stories – a collective narrative.

Over time, I started to go butt-dragging crazy over all the garbage I was seeing around me, and was required to carry. The '*we are right and everyone else is wrong*' and the '*we have always done it this way*' attitudes were so hurtful to my spirit and shattering to the lives of others, especially those *outside* the institutional church, which made them feel as if they had some kind of contagious virus that would destroy the sterilized nature of the institutional church if they were not scrubbed clean before they came in – the funny thing is, those *outside* the church feel those *inside* the church are the ones with the virus. I felt like I was in a bad episode of *The Walking Dead*,[28] defending the prison from the Zombie onslaught; where those outside the church needed the protection from the Zombies within.

---

[28] Just so you know, there is no such thing as a "bad" episode of The Walking Dead.

Not being raised in the church, I was insulting by the "*us vs. them*" teachings and thought patterns. I started to think (*I know, silly me, how dare I think*), 'If they talked that way about those *outside* the church, how did they talk about me before I came in?' Over time I realized the institutional church placed too much emphasis on what we *must believe*, generally ignoring, or simply giving lip service to, how we should be *following* the Naked Jesus. For most, if not all, of them the idea of following meant simply believing, having faith in this Jesus® they created – and not much else.[29]

What I discovered to be so hurtful to my spirit, to my journey in faith, was that every time I had a question one of the Gate Keepers, the *guardians of the institution*, without fail, would snap my head off just for asking the questions. All my

---

[29] I am always amazed at the number of institutional churches that desire me to submit a resume to be their Pastor, only to be rejected because they fear that I would bring "too much" change.

questions were answered with trite company answers like,

Trust the Pastor, after all **HE** *is the Pastor,* or *To truly*

understand you need to get right with Jesus®.[30] If I had a

question concerning something they were doing, or something

that was said, I was made to feel like I wasn't on the faith

trajectory *they* wanted for me. It never failed: any doubt or

question I had was always my fault because I didn't just go

along with the program, (*shut up and drink the Kool-Aid*). I

started to think that I must not be right with the Divine – I

was a heretic – because I entertained such silly questions or

doubted the traditional teachings of the institutional church. I

fell into the trap that I was not right, and self abuse

concerning my faith too hold of my soul. In some cases, they

ignore my questions all together.

---

[30] To be honest, they were right – the questions I asked did not jive with
their understanding of Jesus® and I needed to get right with the Naked
Jesus.

I soon came to realize that the institutional church used Jesus® as a weapon against anyone who disagrees with them. I'm not sure which pissed me off the most, getting canned answers, being abused by others, seeing others being abused or being ignored, but I grabbed my arm-floaties, swam in the shallow end, and played the corporate game — something about eating.

I was uncomfortable with the idea that Jesus® was only for those who said the magic word, prayed the magic prayer, danced the magic dance, bought the company line, or had the ability to duck when the weapon of abuse came out; that Jesus® was only for those who had the secret password, knew the secret handshake, and know how to use the super-secret decoder ring designed to help you understand the *true* hidden meaning behind the collective narrative. That was a twisted and inconsistent teaching of the Naked Jesus I did not want to follow. Still, arm-floaties on, I played the corporate game, and kept swimming.

I worked hard to get my propers, the right credentials. I attended Drew Theological Seminary, received my Master of Divinity, and then went on to pastor, plant and rejuvenate several institutional churches before earning my Doctorate at George Fox University. In all that time, in all the institutional churches I pastored, I kept asking the same questions, kept focusing on the teachings of the Naked Jesus, kept trying to bring life to the people I felt I was called to serve and my denominational leaders. I tried to share the aromas I was inhaling out of the collective narrative and the Naked Jesus, but the slime was just too great. My time at Drew and George Fox gave me the voice I needed to stand my ground and grow a pair. I still played the corporate game, but at least I lost the arm-floaties.

I soon asked myself, "*Self, how crazy are you? How many times do you need to get your ass kicked in that bar before you realize you shouldn't go back?*" Eventually, I started to grasp the meaning of the corporate game, the abuse that seemed to give a twisted masochistic joy to those around me and no longer wanted to swim in the shallow end of the pool. Tired of getting my ass kick in that bar, it was time to move on. I started to get out of the shallow end – slowly at first (*that darn eating thing again*).

The last straw came when I was hit in the back of the head with a beer bottle – or was it the Divine slapping me in the back of the head? Either way, I realized many didn't want to follow the Naked Jesus. They wanted to live life sleeping peacefully in their institutional church, smiling and singing meaningless songs for the Jesus® they created, the one who did not ask them to actually change, actually move off the pews, actually put their faith into their lives, actually put skin

in the game or actually do something with the faith they

claimed. So, after the swelling went down and I got the

stitches removed (*beer bottles hurt*) I decided I would teach

the Naked Jesus and let the chips fall where they may,

forgoing the eating thing.

Fed up, I pushed aside the corporate game. I climbed out of

the *shallow end* of belief, and jumped into the *deep end* of

follow.

Dealing with my personal *Post Traumatic Church Syndrome,*[31]

I began my journey out of what many call *Christianity* into the

deeper waters of the teaching of the Naked Jesus. It was at

that point, standing on the diving board of the adult pool of

---

[31] If you suffer from PTCS, and believe me this is very real, here is a group
of others dealing with the same – check them out, a great group of people
seeking healing: https://www.facebook.com/groups/PTCSgroup/

my faith walk, I realized this is some very scary shit; I had to jump in and learn to swim without the arm-floaties. But I knew I couldn't go back down, back to the shallow end; those arm-floaties chafe. I overcame that nasty habit of eating and decided to trust in the Divine.

Standing on the diving board looking down at the deep end, I knew believing in the Jesus® others pushed on me would make me bat-shit crazy, more bat-shit crazy then I already was. I needed to jump, but the board was high and I was scared shitless. Standing on the edge of the board made me uncomfortable – uncomfortable *in a good way* – but for my sanity I needed to be there. To walk a faith journey that would openly change me internally, I had to get past the Jesus® dressed by others to find and follow the Naked Jesus. I stripped naked and jumped.

In the moment I jumped, arm flailing, leg kicking, loud high-pitch screaming, free fall, semi-creative belly-flop (*I am not a good diver!*) and realized the grace, peace, forgiveness, and freedom one has in the Naked Jesus. I realized what the Naked Jesus was sharing when he spoke of the birds in the field being "*free and unfettered.*"[32] When I felt this absolute freedom, I knew I could walk closer to the Divine. I gave up the corporate game, embraced the Naked Jesus and learned to swim.

SPLASH, I made it, and the water was not cold at all.

---

[32] Matthew 6

CHAPTER THREE:

[To see the Naked Jesus, You Have to Get Naked]

 I know, getting naked is gross – right? But to truly grasp your backstory, as I needed to grasp mine, you need to get naked.

When this book was just a twinkle in my eye, I was sitting at a coffee shop with a friend. During our conversation he asked what my next book was going to be about and I shared a limited overview (*keep in mind it was still a twinkle*). He liked what I was sharing, and said, "That's great, we need books like that. What are you calling it?" I replied, "I am thinking of calling it *The Naked Jesus*."

> **I STARTED BEING REALLY PROUD OF THE FACT THAT I WAS GAY EVEN THOUGH I WASN'T.**
> - Kurt Cobain

Well, you would have thought I said, '*You get the nails, I'll get the wood, and let's find this Jesus guy.*'

Needless to say, he was not overly excited about the proposed title (*not excited* is kind of an understatement). I think he said something like, '*Dude, that's gross – you should find a better title. I don't want to see Jesus naked – you're sick.*' [33]

After going home to change my coffee stained shirt, all I could think was, '*I so want the Naked Jesus. I am tired of all the trappings we place on the Jesus® we say we follow. I just want the plain, naked, unabridged Jesus and want to change my life to fit that narrative.*'

---

[33] As the cover for the book was being designed and I shared some versions on Facebook, he emailed me and told me that the cover was "gross" and that he would be praying for me and he hoped no one purchased the book. The funny thing for me is that, the ideas he liked, it's the cover and the title he did not like – talk about judging a book by its cover.

It never seems to fail; just using the term *naked* sends some people into some sort of *weird cosmic panic mode*.

Culturally, this idea of seeing *anything* naked is filled with massive taboos; never mind seeing a person naked – or Jesus naked for that matter. One friend was concerned what the cover would look like. He was afraid that I would put Jesus on the cover with all his *junk* hanging out. I told him that I like that image, because we need to have all our *junk* hanging out to truly see what needs to be changed in our lives.

If we look at the recording of John in the *New International Version* of the collective narrative we read:

> *When the soldiers crucified Jesus, they took his clothes, dividing them into four shares, one for each of them, with the undergarment remaining.*

This garment was seamless, woven in one piece from top to bottom.[34]

Given that the soldiers had Jesus garments (all his garments), it would seem, to me and others, that Jesus was completely naked.[35] It was not uncommon for the Romans to scourge and crucify a man naked. Knowing that the Naked Jesus was truly naked for all to see shows me, we too must get naked for the entire world to see – we must stand exposed – open and honest.

A friend told me that it would have been an insult to have Jesus hanging naked on the cross; it would have violated Jewish Law. My response was, "*And this would matter to the*

---

[34] John 19:23-24

[35] According to CBN (and I never thought I would ever quote anything from CBN) Rick Renner wrote, "*According to Roman custom, the soldiers who carried out the crucifixion had a right to the victim's clothes. Jewish law required that the person being crucified would be stripped naked. So there Jesus hung, completely open and naked before the world, while His crucifiers literally distributed His clothes among themselves!*" http://www.cbn.com/spirituallife/onlinediscipleship/easter/renner_crucified.aspx: Accessed 5/10/2014

Romans how?" The Idea that Christ was crucified, and crucified naked, speaks volumes to how the he was exposed to the world, in shame and suffering. The nakedness of Christ on the cross reveals, to me, a body so disfigured by scourging and beatings that all who viewed him would be repulsed at the sight.

But Western eyes (and culture) don't like to see other people naked, no, no, no, no, no — well, alright, we do but we call that *porn* and we tell no one we look; after all, *we only buy Playboy for the stories, right?*

Anything to do with being naked, or any mention of a body part, sends many people into some sixth dimension of moral weirdness. I believe it was Clemet XIII who covered all the naked statues in the Vatican with fig leaves, and had all the paintings in the Vatican painted over to cover "the private parts."[36] Interestingly enough, we are kind of comfortable with the word *nude*, but *naked* seems a bit edgier.

Talk about living on the edge. One day, not long ago, I was hanging with a group of people to just talk; we gather about once a month and just share thoughts and ideas about theology, the world, sports, weather, and what will happen on the next season of The Walking Dead.[37] Some of us have known each other for years, and some are new to our little gathering because we invite people all the time.

As one of the new guys started to approach the group, my friend Mark shouted out, in his best *gangsta* voice (*well, in the best gansta voice a white IT Exec, Princeton Grad from San Jose can muster*) said, "*Yo, you be dick!*"

---

[36] For an interesting read on how the church hid the "private parts" check this site out: http://albertis-window.com/2013/05/a-timeline-of-early-modern-censorship/: Accessed 5/10/2014

[37] Yes, I am obsessed with The Walking Dead.

Susan, one of the newer members in our little gathering went ballistic. She started to rail on Mark as we all stood in shock. She quoted scripture after scripture, some I never heard before (*to be honest, I think she made some of them up*), and started to explain how gross he was. She was, to say the least, mad and disgusted with Mark and his statement. As she was ranting on, our new friend stood alongside Mark wondering what the heck was going on. When Susan finished, shaking her head in disgust, Mark looked at her and said, "*Susan, this is my friend Dick Williams.*"

Susan, like most people, see being naked as a *reflexive property*[38] of our faith, where *sin=skin*. We like to place people into categories, but when someone is naked, we have

---

[38] The property that $a = a$. It is one of the equivalence properties of equality.

a hard time categorizing.[39] Being naked is the great equalizer

(*to some degree*). Clothes show us what people do for a

living, where they stand in our society, or if they are rich or

poor. When we remove clothes, we lose our cultural

classification system, and the institutional church likes to put

people into categories – I mean really, how will you know who

will give the most money if you can't judge them by the

clothes they wear.

I love that the Naked Jesus got this, that clothes hinder us

and place us in certain social classes. In Matthew's recording

of events, the Naked Jesus said:

> "*If you decide for God, living a life of God-worship,
> it follows that you don't fuss about what's on
> the table at mealtimes or whether the clothes in
> your closet are in fashion. There is far more to
> your life than the food you put in your stomach,*

---

[39] Notice I did not say it was impossible to do so.

more to your outer appearance than the clothes you hang on your body."[40]

If you think you do not judge people by how they dress, think of a teen in your community with his or her pants sagging below the butt. What do you think? What comes to your mind? Do you assume *gang member*? *Sloppy teen*? – even though you have no proof. We justify our views by saying, "*If they don't want to be seen as a gang member, they should pull up their pants.*" We judge by what we see.

Many in America hold fast to a Victorian notion that nudity is somehow wrong, somehow bad. According to Wikipedia,[41] "*During the Enlightenment, taboos against nudity began to grow and by the Victorian era, public nakedness was*

---

[40] Matthew 6:25-26

[41] Yes Senator, I am willing to quote Wikipedia and give it credit for the quote.

considered obscene."[42] I always found it funny that nudity became such a taboo during the Age of Enlightenment; you would have thought that it would have been seen as something cool. I don't want to spend a great deal of time talking about the History of nudity – you can do your own reading to get that bit of info – but I do want to say that because of this taboo on nudity, just mentioning a Naked Jesus (*even though the term is a metaphor to some degree*) sends a shiver down the spine of some of my more conservative friends, and to be honest with you, I see that as a good thing.

I want to know the Naked Jesus who is real, not the Jesus® covered in clothes others desire him to wear. Even though, like my friend, people realize the term *Naked Jesus* is a metaphor (maybe more than a metaphor), some just can't get

---

[42] http://en.wikipedia.org/wiki/History_of_nudity

past the whole *naked* thing. To them, I have just one thing to say: *Get Over It*.

Many like the Jesus® they have, so they don't need, or want, a Naked Jesus. They want to dress Jesus® like they dress, they want to change Jesus® to fit their desires and needs – and not change themselves to be more like the Naked Jesus. After all, we are independent thinkers who firmly believe that when Jesus® walked the earth he had to think just like us. Our Jesus® must have had the same morality we have, the same view of the world as we do, the same political stance that we hold – so we strive hard to make our own personal Jesus®.[43] Our misconception that all of history must be the same as the history we, or our parents, lived is misguided at

---

[43] I'll have you know, it is taking everything I can pull from my inner theologian not to mentions Depeche Mode's, *Personal Jesus*.

best. We are only able to share, with any honesty, the history we have lived. Anything else is a narrative of perceptions.

Too many people try to fit the Naked Jesus into the perceptions of the historical collective narrative they see as right, instead of fitting their lives into the Naked Jesus' teachings; we want the Jesus® that fits our view of the collective narrative, instead of inviting the Naked Jesus to explode our view of the collective narrative and move us in a new direction.

Jesus® should be the Naked Jesus and we should change to meet him, not change him to meet us. Many *read into* the Naked Jesus so they can create a Jesus® to fit their perception of their world's narrative, personal needs, and desires. The problem with this is that there are far too many personal narratives. When we create a Jesus® we like, based on our personal narrative, we get the Jesus® we deserve, not the Naked Jesus who moves us.[44] But, if you allow the collective narrative to speak to you through the Naked Jesus you will find that you change, and that in and of itself is pretty exciting.

Keeping this an open and honest book, I must admit that what I write might be dressing the Naked Jesus in my clothes. For this process to work, I need to know that my clothes won't fit the Naked Jesus and be willing to take off my own clothes to journey with a Naked Jesus. So, I ask myself three very important questions:

If the Naked Jesus looks like me, why follow?
If the Naked Jesus acts like you, why should I care?

---

[44] My Editor added a little side note for me on this sentence. He wrote, "The other problem is that I get a Jesus as fucked up as I am and how is that Jesus supposed to be able to save me? If _MY_ Jesus could save me, I wouldn't be in this mess! :)"- I just had to add it.

If the Naked Jesus fits neatly into your political views, why change?

Before we can see the Naked Jesus, we have to get naked ourselves. Remember, as I stood on the diving board getting ready to jump, I needed to remove my clothes – my preconceptions – and stand naked on the board. We all need to get naked and put ourselves out there, letting the Divine take hold of our lives, and get ready to dive. We must get naked and remove our ego from the equation; remember, to jump into the deep end of the pool it is better to be naked, clothes will drag you down, and can even cause you to drown.

To look at my own nakedness seems, well, not very interesting. Like most of us, I don't like my body. When we are naked, we see our scars, our wrinkles, our sags, our cheese, our imperfections and our fat rolls; when we are naked we see all the problems we think we have with our bodies, and we just don't like that. But, we all need to strip away the taboos and social mores the world places upon us; we need to be ready to explore out past and our issues and open our lives to others. Jesus says, "*By opening up to others, you'll prompt people to open up with God, this generous Father in heaven.*"[45] I needed to strip away all the crap placed upon me by others, and myself: the expectations, the past, the present, the names, the idea of what does and doesn't make me human and simply look deep into my core, the core the Divine created.

To see the Naked Jesus, I needed to bare all my faults, all my misgivings, all my personal issues and hang-ups to the world. I needed to be willing to stand before others and reject the *fucked-up* me the world created, be the open, honest, flawed, hurt, alone, searching, twisted, shameful, healing, reaching,

---

[45] Matthew 5:16

seeking, wondering, questioning, giving person I had become, and ask myself, '*Is this the me the Divine created, or is this the me the world created?*' and be OK with who I was at my core. I needed to put aside my ego, my desires, and invite the Divine to shine through me so I could be open to the world around me. To find the Naked Jesus, I needed to be released from the crap the world placed upon me, and accept *the me* the Divine created.

Wait, there's more (*you did see that coming, right?*). I also needed to stand where I was and accept the Naked Jesus I found – even if I didn't like what was revealed. I needed to be willing to accept the Naked Jesus who stood before me, not the Jesus® I desired to create in my own thoughts, the Naked Jesus who accepts me for who I am, not the one who demands I fit the ideas of others. If I stood naked before the Naked Jesus and said, "*Take me as I am,*" I needed to be willing to stand before that same Naked Jesus and say, "*I am willing to accept you for who you are.*" I needed to see the Naked Jesus who does not shame me into changing, but the one who loves me into changing – without shame, judgment, anger, demands, or guilt. I needed to be uncomfortable with some of the teachings of the Naked Jesus, because in my *uncomfort* I was able to see the true me. I needed to be challenged by those teachings. I needed to follow those teachings. I needed to realize that if I wasn't challenged, if I wasn't convicted, if I wasn't asked to change my views, I was looking deeper into my own personal views than into the Naked Jesus.

For me to accept the Naked Jesus I needed to be willing to stand before my naked self with the same love, compassion, and acceptance Jesus had for me and share them with others regardless of what the world thought or me. I needed to accept *the me* the Divine created, *the me* the Divine loves, and move forward from that point into the lives of others.

While standing before my naked self, accepting *the me* created by the Divine, I started to ask myself some questions:

Why should I change my worldview?

Why do I need to seek the Naked Jesus?

Why do I desire to stand before him?

Do I even have the right to seek the Naked Jesus?

Am I worthy of seeing the Naked Jesus?

Do I like what I see in my life?

Can I actually do everything the Naked Jesus tells me to do?

Would I be willing to follow, no matter the direction?

Can I live the life the Naked Jesus calls me to live?

Am I willing to invite change into my life and faith journey?

Will this change cause me to do things differently in my life?

The questions were, and are, endless.

Like most people, I have been taught that I am unworthy to seek the Naked Jesus, I am unworthy to walk in his sandals, to think as he thinks, to dance as he dances, to love as he loves, to care as he cares, to forgive as he forgives. Yes, like most, I hid behind the Jesus® others created and clothed. I hid behind my beliefs because it was easier than looking for the Naked Jesus. I knew if I went looking, my world would change and I would be called to follow – I would be challenged in ways that would change me forever.

But, it is in the *just as I am* – just as I was created – that I could, should, and even must connect to the Naked Jesus. It is in our brokenness, our faults, and our humanity that we crave the Naked Jesus – the Naked Jesus who is as he is, and not as I, or others, desire him to be – because that Jesus®, the manufactured Jesus®, is of no value; he is cheap and limited. I am reminded of the words the Naked Jesus shared in

Matthew's recording of the collective narrative, "*You're blessed when you're content with just who you are—no more, no less. That's the moment you find yourselves proud owners of everything that can't be bought.*"[46]

The first step in knowing the Naked Jesus is getting naked yourself and sharing the deepest parts of your life with yourself and others. This is easier said than done. To do this, we need to start to think very differently, we need to redesign our Neuronet...

---

[46] Matthew 5:5

CHAPTER FOUR:
[Developing a New Neuronet]

For me to truly understand how my backstory defined who I was, how I needed to get naked, I needed to take a look at how I thought about the world, myself and others. For you to know your backstory, to get naked and truly understand how everything connects, you need to know how you think — how things connect in your mind. Before we see and understand the Naked Jesus and how to stand naked before him, ourselves and each other, there is a very important step...

> **THE ONLY CREATURES THAT ARE EVOLVED ENOUGH TO CONVEY PURE LOVE ARE DOGS AND INFANTS.**
> - Johnny Depp

We need to define a new neuronet.

What?

I know, it sounds like something out of a *bad* Sci-Fi picture from the 50's, but hear me out (or, *read me out*) – and yeah, can be weird, but not as weird as you think.

This may come as a shock to you, but we all live out our lives in multiple realities; there is no one single reality. Some of those realities we create in our minds and some of those realities others create for us. Either way, our reality is a perception of what is and is not real. We truly do not live in a *reality* – we live in our *perceived reality*.

If we ask the question, *What is real?* I'm pretty sure we can separate what we think is real from what we think is not real and come to a seemingly strong conclusion. Yet I wonder if we can, because "*real*" is a perception. While we think we know what is, and isn't, real we have to be honest with ourselves and say we don't know until we are open to reconnecting our neuronet in relation to what we think and what others have told us.

Let me see if I can explain this with a few examples of what we perceive as real versus what is real.

We define our reality with bits and pieces of information we receive through life, from both observations and conversations. We connect all those bits and pieces together and develop new ideas, new creations, and new directions – and create what we think of as our reality. Sometimes, when we look closely at those bits and pieces we think make sense, we find they don't connect, so we force them to connect. We fill in the blank spaces with what we think should fit based on other past experiences.

Think of it this way. When I say *Humpty Dumpty*, what do you see in your minds-eye?

Think about it for a few seconds.

Get a picture of *Humpty Dumpty* in your mind's eye –

Got it?

Good.

Think of this, nowhere in the nursery rhyme does it say *Humpty Dumpty* is an *egg*. But I bet when you pictured Humpty Dumpty in your mind, you pictured an egg sitting on top of a wall; or, if you are as sick as I am, you pictured him in pieces on the ground. You see, you have a preconceived idea of who *Humpty Dumpty* is based on the bits and pieces you picked up along your life journey (*your perceived reality*). You simply trusted what others told you, or how an artist expressed Humpty Dumpty. In that, you made your image of Humpty Dumpty real; we do this with the Naked Jesus all the time. We base our understanding of who the Naked Jesus is based on what others tell us.

We always claim we need to touch, taste, hear, smell, or see something to determine if it is real or not, but reality is a perception and not something that needs a physical presence; our ability to determine reality via our senses is defined by a perception of reality, not the item in and of itself. Let's look at another example.

Is money real?

OR

Is money a perception we made real?

Is a $50 bill truly worth $50? What gives it the value of $50? What is the difference between a $1 bill and a $100 bill? They are both the same size, the same material is used to make them, almost the same amount of ink is used (you need a little bit more for the two zeros). According to the Federal Reserve it costs about $0.06 to print a dollar bill and $0.13 to print a $100 dollar bill[47] – so, what makes one bill have a value of $1 and the other $100?

Nothing.

The difference is our perception of the value, our perception of truth in relationship to money. We place more value on the $100 because there are two zeros after the one. We perceive the addition of zeros as having more value – *the value is not a reality*, but a perception of our reality.

---

[47] http://www.federalreserve.gov/faqs/currency_12771.htm - Accessed 4/22/14

Money only has value because we have come to place value on it. If we stop perceiving the *reality* that money has value, it no longer has value. If we perceive that zeros take away value, the $100 would be less than $1. The same can be said about anything we see around us. Value is based on perception and if that perception changes, we perceive changes in the value.

The Naked Jesus calls us to change our perception of the world around us. To change the perceived value, we need a completely different view of the world – we need to redefine how we think, how we see reality. That requires we redefine, or rewire, our *neuronet*.

Think of a neuronet as a *map*, a map that has been set over time since a person's birth (*maybe even before birth*) to help us define the world around. When we endeavor to do so, we can change the orientation of our neuronet, but only if we are open to the possibility of change. Like a map, we know our starting point, and we may know our ending point, but the points in between we may not know. Our mind fills in those "unknown places" from past experiences.

In Matthew's recording, the Naked Jesus shared, "*You're blessed when you get your inside world—your mind and heart—put right. Then you can see God in the outside world.*"[48] The Naked Jesus is telling us that we need to rethink our neuronet, to remap our neuronet, we need to see the world in a different light; to put it right; because when we do, we will see the Kingdom of the Divine all around us.

Too many believers in the Jesus® perceive the world as *evil*, but when our hearts and minds are set on the Divine, we see

---

[48] Matthew 5:8

the Divine in the world around us; if all we see is evil, we are not looking at the world through the eyes of the Divine. To do that, we have to willing to change the way we think, the way we express ourselves, the way we interact with others, the way we live in the world. If we spend our time seeing only the evil of the world, we have set our neuronet to see evil. When we do, we miss out on all the beauty of the world created by the Divine. By changing our neuronet we change the way we think and see the beauty we were missing. Over my walk with the Naked Jesus I have become a big believer in realizing that what I see and think, I become – if all I see and think about is evil, I will become evil. So, I focus on the Divine, and in that I see the Divine's love all around me.

This map helps us work out certain problems and defines how we see the world. Over time, as neurons in our brains come together to form certain patterns they are trained to think a certain way. The goal of the Divine is to break those patterns, and open our minds to the possibility of wonders.

The idea that we are born broken, sinful, flawed, weak, a nothing, seems to fly in the face of the teachings of the Naked Jesus, but it is one that has been set in our neuronet, our whole life, because of the teachings of the institutional church. When we develop an understanding of our walk based on the Epistle (the letters) of the collective narrative, we pollute the wonders found in the message of hope (the gospels) found in the collective narrative. To move forward with the Naked Jesus we need to focus on the hope.

To change that perception, we need to center on what the Divine has told us. In the eyes of the Divine, we are created in wonder, we are all beautiful with an amazing potential of greatness; we are created in the image of the Divine. When we see ourselves as broken, sinful, flawed, and weak we fall into the trap that we have no value; we start to define the world as broken, sinful, flawed and weak – we see a world without value, we see a Divine without value. When we walk in the light of the Divine we realize that what others define as our brokenness, our flaws and perceived weaknesses are in fact wonderful gifts given to us by the Divine, and we come to embrace the glory of who we are as co-creators:[49] I think it was Einstein who said, '*If you judge a fish but its ability to climb a tree, it fails.*'

We see the reality we perceive as an intricate net of our perceived reality, a reality where the many complexly interrelating parts feed off each other, sometimes leading us

---

[49] Think in terms of Kintsugi – the art of fixing broken clay pots with gold, silver or platinum.

to very weird conclusions. It is, if you will, how we think or, better yet, how we learned to think.

In our current neuronet, we take what we *know* as the truth, stand fast on how we define our current set of beliefs, and have no desire to understand or accept any alternative way of seeing the truth that would cause an overload. When the perceived reality we think is real is called into question, we ignore the new perceptions (*while enforcing the perceptions we think are right*) or we allow for the overload and can change our views of the world. Enforcing what we think we know creates a Jesus® where we are settled and not changed.

In her book *Mindfulness*, Psychology Professor Ellen J. Langer states, "*Nothing we know is truly independent of context,*" meaning everything is contextual; everything is based on a preconceived idea of what we were told, and how we were told to think. Langer adds, "*people confuse the stability of their mindset with the stability of the underlying phenomena.*" Langer is saying that if we hold our current neuronet as *set* we are being *mindless* (her word) but, if we are willing to change our minds and see things in new ways, in new light, we become *Mindful*. To break the bondage of the teachings of the institutional church, we need to embrace the wonders of the Divine and embrace ourselves as wonderfully created in the image of the Divine.

In Luke's recording of events, the Naked Jesus shares that he has come to *"Start a fire on this earth."* He adds, *"I've come to change everything, turn everything rightside-up..."*[50] He came to confront and disrupt the status quo, to rewire our neuronet, to turn us into revolutionaries – because the world

---

[50] Mathew 12:49-53

we see, the world around us, is upside-down. He came with the heart of a revolutionary to help us redefine our brain connections, to turn the way we view the world upside down, which is in reality *rightside-up*. I found, when I open my life to his words, I no longer see the world in black and white but in the myriad colors that create a world worth living in. We no longer see male and female; we no longer see us and them; we no longer see rich and poor; we no longer see straight and homosexual. We see a world redefined by the interaction of the Divine in our lives. Paul understood this. Though Paul misunderstood many other things, he got this one right on the money. In Paul's writings in the collective narrative, he explains that in the Naked Jesus there is no male or female, young or old, rich or poor, free or servant – there is only YOU and the Divine; Paul adds that "*Among us we are all equal.*"[51]

---

[51] Galatians 3:28-29

When we rewire our neuronet to the Divine, we see a revolutionary new world where all are equal in the eyes of the Divine (and each other) and we learn to embrace that change. When we see all as equal, truly equal, we seek only the best for others, because we know they are seeking only the best for us.

This redefining – revolutionizing – of our neuronet will take the connections we have developed over time as "*the right thing to believe*" and turn them on their head, turn them *rightside-up*. When we start to follow the Naked Jesus and we embrace the redirection of our faith journey, we start seeing the world in a very different light: heck, we start seeing the world in light. We care less about who people are sleeping with and instead realize we are to love everyone. We strive not to place on others a perceived moral code the collective narrative never shares, but simply love. We realize that what the culture is telling us is wrong might not be wrong at all. What we think is bad might be good, what we think is wrong might be right, and what we think is helpful might be hurtful; and the reverse of all that is equally true. We move from a cultural worldview to a *Divine Kingdom view of the world*. We help others and place their needs above our own. We move from selfish to selfless.

When we become mindful, we explode beyond the single-minded views that control our current way of thinking. For this to happen, we need to rethink the world around us – if you will, we need to return to the mind we had as a child.

I think it was the Naked Jesus who said, "*Truly I tell you, unless you change and become like little children, you will never enter the kingdom of heaven.*"[52] Oh, yeah, it was the

---

[52] Matthew 18:3

Naked Jesus who said that. If you think about that, it gets deeper. You see, the *Kingdom of Heaven* (the *Kingdom of the Divine*) is all around us, and the Naked Jesus is saying, "Change the way you think and perceive the world you live in now."

When I opened my life to expanding my neuronet, I opened my world to the possibility I, and all others, are part of the Divine and I saw that following the Naked Jesus was central to my faith journey.

Many take comfort in believing *they* know the truth and therefore ignoring alternative ideas (*they are Mindless*). This may bring comfort, but it also brings about stagnation and it never brings the freedom to develop changes in our neuronet required to make the changes in our behavior, our environment, and our understanding of the Divine in our lives.

If we are willing to refocus our thoughts and our *knowing*, we are open to the possibilities of the Divine (*we become Mindful*). This is freedom: freedom of choice, freedom of interpretation and freedom to live in the moment. Freedom is knowing that when we connect to the Divine in amazing ways, our lives become richer and we enrich the lives of others.

This may sound strange (*I know it sounds anti-American*), but in redefining my neuronet, standing on the diving board getting ready to jump, I came to the conclusion that I have no desire to control my life. I am willing to be open to the plan the Divine has for me. I have no desire to be a *rugged individual American male* who is in control of everything around him. I trust in the Divine's path for me. In my experience – and I know this holds for many of you – when I take control of my life, I screw it up every time and big time at that. My macho individualism is not something I desire to live by.

It is simple. I have no desire to be the Naked Jesus; I desire to follow the Naked Jesus. The Naked Jesus never says *be me* but he does say *follow me*. Following the Naked Jesus gives life to an energy that liberates all of humanity from the crap around us; we are free to love others, free to embrace others, free to want others, free to need others, free to invite others into our lives and accept the hurt that may come from all this freedom. This energy is a force that centers our existence, encourages action to emerge from our hearts, and sets us on a journey where we desire to actually do something to help others. When we follow the Naked Jesus, our desire is to put his teachings into action – so in that sense, the Naked Jesus is experienced as we follow. If this is to happen, if we are going to live in the energy of the Divine, we need to make some rather new and exciting connections in our neuronet that will rewire the circuit board of our faith connections. In remapping our brain to grasp the Divine, we need to be ready for a new enlightenment, a new awakening, a new revitalization of our faith journey. We need to expand and redesign our neuronet. Think of it this way: our faith is defined and controlled by a *Faith Intranet*, a small, controlled collection of connected thoughts, ideas, beliefs, and practices that can blind us to the power, grace and love of the Divine. We need to explode beyond the comfort of the *Intranet* and move the discussion of our faith into the dangerous waters of the *Internet*. In doing so, we start to rethink what it means to be a *Christian*.

This leads us to ask ourselves, *What is a Christian*?

CHAPTER FIVE:

[What is a Christian?]

When I say, *I seek to follow the teachings of the Naked Jesus*, I am speaking of my new neuronet of faith, a *rethinking* of what it means to be a believer. Many who still operate under the old operating system are asking 'Doesn't that make you a *Christian*?' That's a

> **WHAT'S MONEY? A MAN IS A SUCCESS IF HE GETS UP IN THE MORNING AND GOES TO BED AT NIGHT AND IN BETWEEN DOES WHAT HE WANTS TO DO.**
> *- Bob Dylan*

fair question, but it is also forces us to think in an old paradigm of who is right, and who is wrong. Let me start by describing what I mean by *a Christian*.[53]

What is a *Christian*?

---

[53] I want to be careful here. I have no desire to travel into some weird zone where we think we have to correct others. When we follow Jesus, our actions will *show* the difference.

Many believe they are *Christians* because they claim to *believe* in Jesus®, because they profess Jesus® as *their personal Lord and Savior*. But what the heck does that mean? You *believe* in Jesus®? In what way? Besides, what is this *'personal lord and savior'* stuff? I mean really, what does any of that mean? Does that mean I will see you feeding the hungry, caring for the poor, giving water to the thirsty, touching those in need of human contact or does that mean you will simply go to church each Sunday, and send a check so others can do the fun stuff? Does that mean you are covered in what you see as forgiveness when you treat people in ways no human should treat another? Does it mean you have the *right* moral code that all others should live by?

When people say stuff like that, it comes across as spewing corporate sound bites; they have no meaning – it sounds like they are saying, '*I want to buy the world a Coke.*'

One of the local Pastors I know told me the first question we must ask everyone we meet is, "*Are you saved?*" Really? That is the first question we should ask? Really? Instead, let the first question be, "*How are you today?*" and truly listen when they share. The Naked Jesus never asked anyone he met, "*Are you saved?*" But then again, this is the same Pastor who walked into the house of a family that just lost their son and said, before anything else, "*I hope he was saved.*"

I'm not sure *believing* means much of anything, or at least, it does not mean what they think it means;[54] James tells us this in his letter when he writes, "*even demons believe.*"[55] So, when you tell me *you believe*, all I can do is think, "*Isn't that special?*"

---

[54] Echoing the worlds of Inigo Montoya in the *Princes Bride*, "You keep using that word. I do not think it means what you think it means."
[55] James 2:19-20

In my struggle to develop a good definition, my good friend Jim Palmer[56] nails it and gives a wonderful definition of what the institutional church, and what a "Christian" looks like. For many:

- Church is a place, a location, a building.
- Christianity happens in services, classes, meetings, events, and programs.
- What people need most is good information about God.
- "God's work" needs organizational or corporate infrastructure.
- The more control the better; no telling what people will do if left to themselves.
- It's best you let us decide how to use and distribute your money.
- Depend on us for the spiritual formation of your children; we are trained.
- The bigger the church, the better.
- People are more valuable and spiritual based on how often they are there and how much they give.

---

[56] http://jimpalmerblog.com/

- Relationships happen in group meetings.[57]

My friend Ceamdon Michael adds, "*Church is a time slot.*"

Institutional churches are churches were abuse, control and exclusion have been *institutionalized* within the fabric of their being and where they have become religious *commercial enterprises.* Christians are those who support such a reality.

The word *Christian* comes from the Greek word *Christianos* and originally meant the person claiming to be a Christian was considered a *follower of the teachings of Christ,* a revolutionary following the teachings of the Naked Jesus. Over time, we have redefined it to *believing in a religion.*

The idea of being a follower may have been the reality 2,000 years ago in Antioch, but I'm certain it that is not what it

---

[57] http://jimpalmerblog.com/2012/10/02/10-implied-messages-of-institutional-church-because-the-medium-is-the-message/ accessed 4.16.14

means today. Today, being a Christian means you believe in
Jesus® and see him as your personal lord and savior –
nothing more. Well, it may mean that you need to go to
church on Sundays, and your life is defined by some particular
moral code developed on a whim.

I know so many people who call themselves *Christians* who
aren't even close to following the teachings of the Naked
Jesus.[58] Most of them find a home in the political right and
find themselves hosting tea parties and demanding their views
be upheld as *the only true way to see Christianity*. Many of the
right fall into this reality, but I know many on the *left*, or the
progressive side, who feel the same way – both are wrong.

Those on the right play the *I believe, I go to church, I asked
Jesus to forgive my sins* card which, if you're playing poker, is

---

[58] Before you get all pissy over that statement – please note the "many"
and not "all."

a pretty crappy hand to hold; those on the left hold an equally horrid hand in the game, but they tend to ask the right questions.

These Christians are really asking, *what is in this for me?* The institutional church's version of Christianity is a *cultural Christianity*, a consumer based Christianity where they focus on a narcissistic view of believing: *What can the church do for me? How is the Pastor going to feed me today?* They are deaf to the *missional* questions of a follower of the Naked Jesus: *What will I do for my community of faith? What can we do for our community at large? How can I serve others today?* Both sides have this issue; it is just that the right shouts it louder. If all we do is consume, all we can share with others is our waste, our excrement. We take all the nutrients for ourselves and all we have left to share is human waste.

I have found that calling ourselves *Christian* has had little to do with *following* Christ and everything to do with being a *good church person,* one who holds moral superiority over another. When I started to speak about *following* – following the teachings of the Naked Jesus – I get blank stares from many in the institutional church, as if I was from another planet. When those in the institutional church speak of *following*, they are not talking about following; they are talking about writing a check so others can do the dirty work, or just talking about what "those people" should do (never realizing that *they* are the *those* they speak of) to make themselves right with Jesus®. I'm not sure when it happened – I'm pretty sure it doesn't matter when – but we've changed the meaning of *Christian* from one who is concerned with *doing something with their faith*, to one concerned with *appearances, consumerism, and having someone else do the work*. We made a dramatic move from following (*action*) to believing (*words*) – to embrace the changes in our world I have come to realize, we need far more action, not so many words.

The Naked Jesus told us others will know we're his followers by our love, not by our words. We have shifted that to mean, *others will know we are Christian by how loudly we shout WE LOVE JESUS;* or *how many 'Christian' bumper stickers we have on our car.*

We have come to a point in our collective history where we define Christianity less by following and more by how we look in attending our church and pretending to be *a good Christian*. If we do use the term *follow* in this context, it usually refers to how we project ourselves: how we dress, how we cut (or not cut) our hair, how the programs we develop to serve our needs, how nice our buildings look, or how new our hymnals are, how cool our worship services come across. Unfortunately, in the years since the term was first coined, it has lost a great deal of its meaning to the world around us and is often used for someone seen as overly religious or has a perceived high moral code but who may or may not be a *follower* of the Naked Jesus.

I could spend hours trying to define what it means to be a Christian, but how do those who claim to be Christians define what it means?

Adrian Warnock, in his book *Raised with Christ*, says, "*A Christian is someone who believes in the physical resurrection of Jesus Christ, and lives in light of the implications of that event.*" Limiting the defining criteria for being a Christian to one event (*no matter how important*), to one moment in time, reduces the role of following to upholding momentary belief.

When that happens, we are no longer following what the Naked Jesus told us to do, we focus, instead, on the event. The Naked Jesus tells us if we are in his camp, we need to follow.[59] Limiting what it means to be a follower to believing Jesus® rose from the dead seems shallow and rather one sided; because in the Naked Jesus there is a multifaceted depth one needs to understand and seek to follow. The idea is to not only believe in the resurrection, but to embrace how the resurrection changes your life and moves you to action; I know too many Christians who are living in the resurrection, but are dead to the hurts, pains and lives of others.

Matt Slick of the *Christian Apologetics and Research Ministry* writes:

> "*So, being a Christian means that you have encountered the true and living God and that you*

---

[59] Matthew 16:24-26

have undergone a change in your heart and soul.
It means that you are not restricted to the Laws of
right and wrong in order to please God because
you cannot please God by what you do. God will
only find pleasure in you through Jesus Christ."[60]

I will admit that I like the idea of *encountering* the Divine, but

Matt's telling us that while we have a changed heart, that

change only helps us believe, not follow. Once again we are

limited to simply believing and not following. Besides, to be

honest with you I get a real bad taste in my mouth when I

read "*God will only find pleasure in you through Jesus Christ.*"

Why? Because the Divine takes pleasure in you, when you are

just being you, regardless of where you're at in life.

I could share other voices, but they all share pretty much the

same words, *believe and all is good.*

---

[60] http://carm.org/christian - accessed on 1/4/14

These definitions – and most I have read – prioritize believing *over* following while Jesus speaks of following, *then* believing.

Both of these definitions seem limited and distant to me, the first limits us to an event and the other limits the reality of the Divine's love for us. Neither speaks of following. Neither says the Divine cares more about our desire to involve ourselves with and open our lives to the poor, the broken, and the hungry, and taking pleasure in us just as we are. The Naked Jesus shares this with us in Matthew's recording of events, "*You're blessed when you're content with just who you are— no more, no less. That's the moment you find yourselves proud owners of everything that can't be bought.*"[61] The Divine loves us for being us. We don't need to say a magic prayer or speak special words to enter some weird club; we are already connected. We are all instruments of the Divine,

---

[61] Matthew 5:5

co-creators in what could be an amazing world – if we truly follow and put our faith into action.

To realize this, to embrace this, we need to be captured by the grace and love offered by the Divine through the Naked Jesus. When we do this, we invite others to see this living grace in us. We realize our journey within the Divine's Kingdom has a single focus. Our primary purpose is TO LOVE.

As co-creators we realize those who meet us must see that love in us, they must meet the risen Christ in us – but to do that we need to interact with others. To the extent we fail to show this love, to live this love, we fail to show others the change the Divine makes in our lives. Without this love, we are no different from those who do not know this love, and we are no better than those in the world who abuse others. This love is not defined by our desire to convert people into Christians, but to love people into Christ.

Our love for the Divine is a reflection of the Divine's love for us, not based on beliefs but on being ourselves and extending ourselves to others with that love.

I have to admit, I hesitated to give a definition of what "is" a Christian because I fear it would come across negative and offend too many people who see it as a good term. It is a label that carries so much negative weight I knew any definition I shared would not be pleasant. But, the question *What is a Christian?* does lead us to another question...

*What makes **you** a Christian?*

Josh McDowell says:

> *"Jesus said that to enter the kingdom of heaven a person must be 'born again' (John 3:3). This consists of an act of the heart in believing Jesus Christ as Lord and Savior. When we were born into the world physically, we were born spiritually dead, and therefore we need a spiritual birth."*[62]

What Josh fails to remember is that Jesus never says we must *believe in him as Lord and Savior to enter the Kingdom of God.* Also, Jesus never said we were born *"spiritually dead."* They are concepts and terms used by the institutional church for control and power.

For the Naked Jesus, the *Kingdom of the Divine* is not something we enter; it is something that exists all around us. We are born into the Kingdom of the Divine. In Luke's recording of the life and ministry of Jesus, Jesus says,

---

[62] http://tinyurl.com/k3s9s9r

> "*The kingdom of God doesn't come by counting the days on the calendar. Nor when someone says, 'Look here!' or, 'There it is!' And why? Because God's kingdom is already among you.*"[63]

Too many in the institutional church claim this only happens when we see ourselves as *Born Again* and – this may sound strange – I somewhat agree, but not in the way they think, *more on that later* (Sorry for the tease, I could not resist).

So, the next question becomes, *Isn't believing important?*

Sure it is – I never said it wasn't – but it does not take the place of following as many in the institutional church *believe*. In reality, I see believing as the end result of following. You can't believe if you do not follow, and if you do not follow you cannot claim that you believe. Most definitions of Christian center more on *belief* (a noun) and less, if ever, on *following*

---

[63] Luke 17:20-21

(a verb). I tend to think many prefer Christianity as a set of beliefs (look at the *What We Believe* page on any church website) because beliefs don't call us to action and, if we're not called to do something with our faith, we can justify our lack of action while claiming to be a Christian.

Most church doctrines list what you must *believe* to be a true Christian. Few (*if any*) list how we are to *act* in following the Naked Jesus. Most (*again, if not all*) churches say *believe in this list* and all will be great. Over my life, I have come to the realization that being a *Follower of The Teaching of the Naked Jesus* is not so much a matter of what you believe, but how you follow the teachings of the Naked Jesus and see how to live in love, grace, forgiveness, and acceptance and care for those marginalized by the culture.

What if, during a web search, you came across a page that

read:[64]

What we believe:
As followers of the teaching of the Naked Jesus we believe...

> We must care for those society has ignored. We
> gather together as often as possible as a community
> of faith and use our time, gifts, and money to help
> those who are in need. Our call is not to determine
> who is worthy of our actions, but to live by the
> teaching that we are to care for the poor, the hurt,
> the broken, the abused, the misunderstood, and the
> marginalized. We are ready, willing, and able to share
> our lives and our funds in the process of helping
> others. We do this in the following ways:

> We gather weekly to cook and distribute food to
> those in and around our community who are
> hungry. We do this, regardless of laws telling us
> not to, because the Naked Jesus told us to feed
> the poor.

---

[64] Check out http://generationsway.com/what-we-believe/ At
GenerationsWay.com this is list is part of our "What we believe" page.
Accessed 4/3/2014

We collect and distribute clothes to those in
need – not by dropping them off to a thrift store
where we get the tax deduction and others have
to buy the clothes, but directly to those on the
street.

We stand ready to give our coat and shirt to
someone who needs them.

We share our time and love to help mend the
broken, the abused, and the marginalized.
Those who society has pushed aside, we
embrace, love, care and help the best we can.

We include the excluded. We welcome all
people, as they are, inviting them into our lives
and into the House of the Divine.

That would be rather interesting. I think it would say a great

deal about the church.

If you tell me you believe in the Naked Jesus, but your belief

does not produce action, it means nothing to me – you see, I

lived in that shadow for a long time. Living as a *Follower of the Teachings of Christ* is everything. I love the way John the Baptizer explains it in Marks recording of the life and ministry of Jesus:

> *"The real action comes next: The star in this drama, to whom I'm a mere stagehand, will change your life. I'm baptizing you here in the river, turning your old life in for a kingdom life. His baptism—a holy baptism by the Holy Spirit— will change you from the inside out."*

When I say *"I am a Follower of the Teachings of Jesus Christ"* I'm saying...

I seek to be changed on the inside, in a revolutionary way.

I seek to live the life the Naked Jesus tells us to live.

I'm uncomfortable with a consumer-based faith.

There has to be more to life than what I see around me.

I have a bunch of questions, and want to ask them all.

I am alright if you do not have an answer, just admit it.

"Why don't we do something together?"

There will be pain, but following the Naked Jesus will be worth it.

Those who simply believe have a narcissistic view of faith; they like *being a believer* because it requires far less work on their part than being a follower and they get to put a sweet little "*Ichthus*" (Christian Fish) on their business cards, or on the back of their car – while cutting people off in traffic;[65] but their faith centers on what they get out of it and not what they give to it. It demotes *being like* the Naked Jesus to *believing in* Jesus®. Since they're not following the Naked Jesus, they can redefine his teachings to fit their lives and beliefs; they don't have to change. But something has to change. They devise spiritual sounding justifications so that instead of being changed themselves, they can redefine Jesus® according to their standards.

---

[65] My Father use to say, "Never trust a guy who puts a Christian fish on his business card. They will lie to you, cheat you and change you twice what they promised all in the name of Jesus."

Over time, many have redefined Jesus as a Republican, a liberal, a conservative, or a Democrat. We ask silly questions like, *What Would Jesus Do?* As if asking such a question actually has meaning to our faith journey. Even worse, we answer the question as if we asked, *What Do I Want Jesus To Do?* or *What Do I want Jesus To Do For Me?* I know this because I lived it and saw it all around me – I still see it.

You see, *belief* says we believe something exists; *following* means we take action because we dance in that existence; we put skin in the game. We follow from a desire to do what the Naked Jesus tells us so belief will develop:

We love – not because we were first loved, but because we are invited to love.
We care for the poor – because we love.
We accept those who are different – and we love them.
We embrace the life changing reality of faith in following.

Many Christians believe and do nothing. James said it best when he wrote:

> "*Do I hear you professing to believe in the one and only God, but then observe you complacently sitting back as if you had done something wonderful? That's just great. Demons do that, but what good does it do them?*"

What seems to grow out of this focus on belief is a faith that talks a great deal, but does very little; we remain the same person we were before we believed. We don't change at all, but we strive to change the Naked Jesus.

Sometimes this is subtle: we think Jesus® is changing us, but in reality we're not changing at all. If we are changing, our faith journey will be uncomfortable and tension will build between the words of the Naked Jesus and our desires.

"*Do you think I came to smooth things over and make everything nice? Not so. I've come to disrupt and confront! From now on, when you find five in a house, it will be— Three against two, and two against three; Father against son, and son against father; Mother against daughter, and daughter against mother; Mother-in-law against bride, and bride against mother-in-law.*"[66]

The Naked Jesus is saying that if we follow him, our world will be turned *rightside up* – because the world we live in is upside down. Those who like living in this *upside down* world will be unhappy with us and we will be unhappy with ourselves as we progress and adjust our worldview to being *rightside up*. We will change our point of view and focus on love, peace, forgiveness, grace, and acceptance. As we change, we hope

---

[66] Luke 12:49-53

to see the world around us change. We hold fast to the teachings of the Naked Jesus and not of Ayn Rand.

With this in mind, we need to ask ourselves:

Do we want the Naked Jesus to change us or do we desire a puppet Jesus® we can pull out when we need it?

SECTION II
[The questions]

In searching for the Naked Jesus, we develop questions; I know because I had a billion of them, and still do. I am certain you developed some questions while reading the first section of this book. Questions like, "*What the heck is this guy smoking?*" and "*Where can I get some?*" I hope to answer some of your questions in this section. Well, maybe not the smoking question so much.

We will start by exploring the collective narrative. Then, we jump into some questions:

Who do you say I am?

Are you tired of this radical Jesus?

Are we there yet?

What are sin, salvation and sacraments?

How about we use the word Koinology?

CHAPTER SIX:
[An Amazing Messy Story]

 For me to truly follow the Naked Jesus, I needed to get the narrative right (*his backstory*), I needed to read the story as an amazing, messy story of hope and love.

To my mind, there is nothing like a good story.

I love a good story. I mean I **_LOVE_** a good story. This could be because most people in my family spun amazing, exciting narratives. I firmly believe that a good story should be exciting, even life

> IMAGINE ALL THE PEOPLE LIVING LIFE IN PEACE. YOU MAY SAY I'M A DREAMER. BUT I'M NOT THE ONLY ONE. I HOPE SOMEDAY YOU'LL JOIN US. AND THE WORLD WILL BE AS ONE.
> - John Lennon

changing. It should make you think. No, a good story should make you dream; it should move you past your current reality.

The telling brings the characters to life in such a way that the reader, or hearer, of the story relates to it and grows from the experience. A good story encompasses the life experience of the person telling it and the person hearing it. When we hear a good story, we become emotionally involved in the characters; we become invested in them. Every good story holds an element of adventure beyond simple entertainment. A good story should open our eyes to possibilities and open our hearts in ways never thought possible. It should open your spirit to express your deepest thoughts. The narrative of the Naked Jesus can do just that, and more.

As the storyteller weaves their enchanting tale it should take you places way beyond your wildest imagination. Such a story will change the way you look at the world, the way you look at yourself, and the way you look at others. For a story to do any of that, it must be shared on its own without others telling you what you should feel, think, or believe about the story. The story needs to stand on its own; *the story must be the story*. So it should be with the story of the Naked Jesus.

Many of the people I have encountered in the church have heard the story, but they have not been changed by it – they have not learned to dream about the possibilities of the story.

Before I share this story with you – actually a collection of stories – I would like to share with you two very important *realities* that should guide our understanding of this collection of stories, this collective narrative.

The first thing to understand about this collective narrative is that the institutional church sees their interpretation of their version of the collective narrative – and the lead character, Jesus® – as the only true version. Any change from their perceived homogeneous story and authorized brand causes great concern among its members who desire to hold strong to the registered trademark. Any, any change to their *Jesus®* *brand* disrupts their corporate model and, as such, forces them to defend the Jesus® they created.

In general, most in the institutional church are lost in their perceived tranquil and monotone expression of the collective narrative. In that, they miss the possibilities of the Naked Jesus found in the naked collective narrative. The Jesus® they created is not the Naked Jesus I searched for and came to know. Because of this I find it hard to connect with their monotone expression of Jesus®. The leaders in the institutional church accuse those who speak out against the Jesus® they created as a rabid lawyer defends a lawsuit. Those who question the institutional version of the collective narrative are accused of painting the institutional church with a wide brush. That may be, but the real issue is that the brushes of those asking the questions are dipped in trays filled with colors and possibilities, while the institutional brushes are dipped in whitewash.

Their brand of Jesus® is centered more on a political journey and less on the collective narrative. To question the presuppositions of the institutional church concerning Jesus®, his perceived collective narrative, or the doctrines and theology that come from those presuppositions causes the institutional church to label the questioner a *Heretic*. Yeah, I accept the heretic label, because I'm more concerned with finding the truth of this amazing collective narrative and less concerned with the labels others give me.

The second important reality is that this collective narrative is not some kind of science book, history book, math book, or political science book, and it is not a psychology or philosophy book. When we view it that way, we do the collective narrative a harsh injustice; we cloud the reality of the collective narrative. That is not to say we ignore the cultural, contextual, and historical aspects of the collective narrative – those are important aspects of the narrative – but the collective narrative was not written to be an account of history, as we understand it. The collective narrative was written to express the Divine's interaction with humanity and humanity's desire to hold this collective narrative to that interaction – how the Divine interacts with all of us. When we view the collective narrative in this light, we see the wider narrative of hope: a narrative where the Divine is interacting with real people, in real times, and in real places, under real situations and those writing the collective narrative are trying hard to grasp that interaction and live in the tensions we find. To wholly embrace the collective narrative for what it is, we need to recognize it as a complex collection of stories that have had a lasting effect on the course of human history – for good or bad. When we see this wider narrative of hope in its cultural context, it reveals its relevance to people today. This requires willingness to question the lenses we have used to filter this collective narrative (our neuronet) and understand how that lens affects our reading. For this to happen, for us to truly grasp the meaning behind the collective narrative, we need to move past the idea that it is a "word for word" infallible document and embrace the narrative given by the individual writers.

While we undertake to know how the wider narrative works in our lives, we are invited to find satisfaction in knowing we will never figure it all out and others will see things differently. Knowing we will never figure it all out should not stop us from trying to understand how the wider narrative of hope fits our lives. We need to wrestle with individual stories to help understand the grand stories of the wider narrative without ignoring or taming the individual stories. The grand stories of the wider narrative are not to be taken literally, word for word, but to be held as a collective narrative in which the human authors are sharing what they perceive the Divine has shared with them at that point in time.

As a final note about the grand stories of the wider narrative, it is designed to change the individual, not the world. The world only changes *when* the individual changes. The wider narrative of hope is not a political hammer to mandate the behaviors of others or place your views of morality upon the lives of those who do not follow the narrative of hope as you do; our faith should guide us, as individuals, and not be forced upon the wider culture. We don't need to build laws and control systems based on our beliefs; we are simply called to live what we believe. We need to see ourselves as players in the collective narrative. As I have said before, this amazing narrative of hope can only change the behavior of the individual person. This narrative of hope that sets us free does not shackle those we disagree with. The narrative of hope frees us to love others, frees us to help those in need, and frees us to care for the marginalized, the broken, and the hurting. We are free to forgive and move forward in our lives. If we see any collective change in the lives of others, it should be in our local Community of Faith. If not, we have lost sight of the words the Naked Jesus speaks about being changed, "*Change **your** life and believe the Message.*"[67]

To grasp this collective narrative, the recording of the events of the life of the Naked Jesus, some people put words to parchment to share with us the stories, thoughts and actions they thought were important for us to understand – the

---

[67] Mark 1:14-15 – emphases added

stories, thoughts, and actions they thought would change our lives and move us to freedom – to see a world with a new expression of faith, love, and grace. Those who shared their views and the views of those who came before them expressed their understanding of the collective narrative in the hopes of changing our lives. To be completely forthright, their recording of events was limited. John, in his recording, shares *"There are so many other things Jesus did. If they were all written down, each of them, one by one, I can't imagine a world big enough to hold such a library of books."*[68] To suggest no other voices can be heard over the mandated cannon seems to ignore the reality that there are other voices who wrote other parts of the collective narrative. Some in the past, others today and still more in the future.

---

[68] John 21:25

Over my faith journey, I have come to the conclusion that we take a poor theological stance when we assume all that was and is contained in the collective narrative, that no new voices will speak to be heard. When we do this, we come to the incorrect conclusion that the Divine is not speaking to us today and only spoke to those in times past. If that is the case, if the Divine is not speaking today, the collective narrative has no real meaning to us today and the narrative of hope is dead. When we hear new voices, we remember that this amazing story is still unfolding, still living. We understand we live in common unity with the collective narrative and the Divine.

Over the past century we have confused this amazing collective narrative – of grace, of love, of forgiveness, of community, of connection, of understanding, of acceptance – with the monocultural, institutional church's story we have woven into the fabric of our culture, a story of self-satisfaction, judgment, exclusion, and control. Many are so connected to the institutional church's story they have lost the ability to see the colors set before them in this amazing collective narrative woven into the mosaic of life. Those in the institutional church see everything dressed in black and white, while the Naked Jesus shares an amazing rainbow of colors, unearthed when we embrace the collective narrative. The Evangelical myth has confused the narrative of hope with a story of control, judgment, demands, magic, separation, and rejection.

So, what is this amazing collective narrative?

This collective narrative takes place in a land outside our ability to understand culturally, yet well within our ability to understand how the story relates to our culture today. It is a land filled with people who see the world differently, yet not

entirely different from the way we see ours. A land where life
was cheap, people had no rights, and freedoms were few and
far between. A place where subsistence living was the norm
and food came at a steep price. A child born into this world
had a rocky start at life and a rough time reaching their first
birthday. You see, in that world, at that time, 25% of all
children died before their first birthday and over 50% died
before their tenth birthday. A child born into this world would
live under the control of an imperial government, the elite, the
powerful, the religious cast, and the wealthy, where the
personal whims and desires of those who held positions of
power and authority were followed without question; and if
they were questioned, death was always the reply. The
chances of a child born into poverty moving out of poverty
were slim at best, if at all possible.

Our story continues with the introduction of our first character, a frightened, scared, single,[69] strong, young woman[70] who found herself in a condition sure to bring death upon her and shame upon her family. This young woman found herself single, pregnant, alone, and wondering what the future would bring. Fear of what could, might, or would happen – given the laws of her culture and the religious views regarding single, young women with child – gripped every fiber of her being. Her fears were real: she was poor, alone, and confused. Believing she was alone, she questioned everything and lived in fear. The same fear and concerns facing many single, pregnant women in our world today.

---

[69] The idea that Mary was not married to Joseph at the time seems to fly in the face of what we think today. We strive to clean-up the collective narrative by saying they were married, but they were not.

[70] Tradition holds that she was a teenager (maybe 13). While this may come from tradition and a cultural understanding, the collective narrative does not share her age.

Into this story came a man.[71] This man was not the hero of the story coming to save the *damsel in distress*. He was not a *Knight in Shining Armor*. He was in fact a simply day laborer,[72] the kind of guy you see standing in the parking lot of your local Home Depot looking for any work he can get to support his growing family. He didn't have a great deal to offer; he too lived in poverty, trying to find work on a daily basis. He was simply a man, a man who loved this young woman and was willing to stand by her side no matter the situation. He knew what was coming to her so, weighing all the possibilities and problems, he took it upon himself (with a Divine nudge) to stand with her and to be present for her. He was willing to

---

[71] Some believe he was much older and died while Jesus was a child. There is no evidence for this either. Since the institutional church had no idea what do you do with the earthly father of Jesus, killing him off in tradition seemed the easiest thing to do.

[72] The word used in Matthew is Tecton and in Mark it is Tekton. Throughout history we have translated this word as "carpenter," but that is not exactly what the word indicates. The word more accurately means a "handy-man" or "Mr. Fix-it," meaning a man who took what jobs he could get.

share his life with her and raise the child as his own, willing to stand firm in his love no matter what came or what others thought, willing to go against the cultural norms of his day and embrace woman and child as his own in love. This man decided to honor his commitment to take this scared young woman as his wife regardless of her current condition, regardless of what others thought.

Into this story, into this land of fear and control, a child was born to a scared, single, loving woman and a grace filled, loving man willing to stand by her. The child entered this world just like most of us: head first, covered in blood and fluids, kicking and screaming, and knowing the abandonment of the internal warmth of his mother's womb only to face a cold world filled with violence and poverty.

Soon after birth, this child was rushed off to a foreign land where he spent most of his youth as an illegal alien. In this foreign land his father could support his new and growing family in conditional safety.

In the land of his birth, the people continued to suffer under the oppressive control of the powerful, the government officials, and the religious leaders. In the land of his birth, the rich got richer, the poor got poorer, and the religious leaders sought to consolidate their power over the people. The broken and marginalized were deemed *unclean* and rejected from the House of the Divine by the religious leaders.

Nevertheless, this collective narrative is one of hope and not fear. Our story continues with the grace and love of the Divine working in this child born into poverty, raised on the margins of society, loved in a blended family with two parents, four brothers, and two sisters, struggling to make ends meet on a daily basis, living most of his childhood outside the land of his birth.

The child grew to become a young adult who would change the world. He became a young adult who would take all his past experiences of being an illegal alien; being raised by a loving, adoptive father and a warm, caring mother; seeing abject poverty in his life and the lives of others; and seeing the broken, the unclean, and the marginalized abused by the religious and political leaders of his day, and introducing crazy, wonderful, teachings into the lives of everyone.

Ideas so crazy, so weird, so life changing, they scared the religious and political leaders of his day. Ideas so crazy, so weird, so different, so life changing, so out of place with cultural *norm of the day*, they blew people's minds. Ideas so crazy, so revolutionary, so scary, that many of the religious and political leaders who heard his voice had a hard time conceiving what he was speaking about. Ideas that would change the way we thought about ourselves, others, and the world around us; even change the way we viewed the Divine's interaction with humanity. Ideas so life changing that the institutions of his day tried to control and subvert them in any way possible. Ideas so amazing that many who came after him tried to temper those teachings to fit their desires, the culture, the government, and the religious institutions forming around his teachings. Ideas so controversial that many in the current incarnation of the institutional church ignored them, because they could not embrace them and still justify their power and placement in culture and over the lives of others; they knew people would see very little, if any, need for the institution itself.

Let me introduce you to this child who grew to become the man his friends called *Yeshua Ben Yosef.* The young man known to his family and friends as *Yeshua*, who we are coming to know, *I call Naked Jesus.*[73]

In the past, we have been told of this collective narrative in a clean, sanitized, and rather boring way. The institutional church doesn't like the reality of the Naked Jesus because, when you know his narrative, you see how messy it can be, messy in a good way for some, but in a not so good way for the institutional church. You see, when we desire to follow the teachings of the Naked Jesus our lives become filled with hurting, abused people looking for connection between themselves, us, and the Divine. Most institutional church people I know tend to not like this because they know messy

---

[73] Yoshua is the Hebrew name of Jesus – Jesus is a the Greek interpretation of his Hebrew name

people can make for a messy Community of Faith; they are ok with connecting people with the Divine, just not with themselves. Besides, living a life where we deal with those hurting, broken, messy people can cause us to question the institution's multi-million dollar buildings and budgets.

For many, the collective narrative of the Naked Jesus has been scrubbed clean, with the removal of all but a few trivial moments of messy – small moments they can handle or overlook. Over time we have taken the messy collective narrative of *Yeshua* and turned it into the sanitized collective narrative of Jesus®...

Over time, we have softened the rough edges of the collective narrative to make the story palatable to those in the institutional church who have never read the story for themselves. We changed the collective narrative to:

(*Before reading the next paragraph, play some sappy contemporary Christian music in the background*)

Into an evil world a sweet, mild, good-natured baby Jesus® was born to a happily married couple in a barn, and placed in a manger on a snowy Christmas morning. Soon, three older men came by to share gifts with the sweet baby Jesus® so we could know that spending billions on gifts each year proves we are worthy of his love. A sweet, mild, kind Baby Jesus® who will forgive you every time you ignore some poor shmuck on the streets looking for a handout of your hard earned money. A blonde haired, blue eyed, white, Christmas card Jesus® who makes you feel all warm and fuzzy inside and never calls you to change or view the world in a different way. That red, white and blue American Jesus® who says greed is good and the poor are just lazy creeps who need to get a job and stop leeching off your hard earned dollars. Yes, that American Jesus® who died for our American way of life, and even tells us to kill those

*who stand opposed to Almighty Capitalism. The
Jesus® whose step-daddy was a carpenter,
because a carpenter is so much more palatable
then a day laborer.*

(*End music*)

Let's be honest. A screaming, messy child born into objective poverty to a young mother and a stepdad standing in the parking lot of a Home Depot is not very clean; it doesn't sell Christmas cards.

The institutional church has no desire to see the human Jesus®: a Naked Jesus who is struck with all the human emotions of the people pushed aside by the church as *unclean* and *unwanted*; a Naked Jesus who, after 40 days in the wilderness, smelled funky and needed to take a bath; a Naked Jesus who needed to go behind a rock every now and then and take care of business. It is so much easier to live with the institutionally created Jesus® who does not challenge us to open our hearts, but calls us to sit fat and happy in our pews (*or chairs*) for one hour on Sunday.

The reality is, it doesn't matter which name you use, *Jesus, Yesha, or Joshua*. What matters is that we seek to see him as he is, not as we desire him to be. What matters is that we move from Jesus® to the Naked Jesus.

To do that, to get a grip on the collective narrative, we need to see the collective narrative for what it is, not for the myths we developed around a sanitized, palatable version acceptable to our contemporary minds. To understand what happened, we need get a hold of those crazy teachings because the Naked Jesus I know is not all that clean and is very willing to get messy with us.

- The Naked Jesus I know sits at the right hand of the plug-chomping, whiskey drinking, foul mouthed biker sitting at the end of the dark, smelly, dirty bar in the bad part of town wondering about life;

- The Naked Jesus I know stands with the day laborers in front of Home Depot and goes on jobs with them;

- The Naked Jesus I know knows from experience what it means to live in poverty and hunger, what it means to be broken and marginalized, and what it feels like to be left out of all *the reindeer games*;

- The Naked Jesus I know stands with the marginalized of our culture, the day laborers, the illegal aliens, those born in blended families, those with different sexual identities, those who are broken, those who live in poverty, and welcomes them all with open arms;

- The Naked Jesus I know stands between the self-righteous, religion spewing, bible thumping church goers with rock filled pockets and the women entering Planned Parenthood Clinics;

- The Naked Jesus I know stands with the marginalized across the street from those carrying signs and chanting against them for their authentic lifestyle;

- The Naked Jesus I know stands hand-in-hand with the unwashed, the unworthy, the untouchable, the unaccepted, the unwanted, and welcomes them with open arms into his house to eat at his table;

- The Naked Jesus I know stands with the abused against personal, corporate, bank, and systemic greed;

- The Naked Jesus I know doesn't give a rat's ass about his reputation or yours;

- The Naked Jesus I know was despised by the religious leaders of his day because he refused to play their corporate games or hold their point of view as right;

- The Naked Jesus I know stands against those who desire to control or exclude anyone from the Divine's Kingdom;

- The Naked Jesus I know is a great lover of humanity and lived from his heart to accept people where they were, not where the religious right wanted them to be;

- The Naked Jesus I know inspires us to live an untamed, crazy, weird, free life where love is the core of our being and forgiveness is the center of our life;

- The Naked Jesus I know taught me to feed the hungry, forgive others, give water to the thirsty, welcome strangers into my home, love my enemy, provide clothes to those in need, and visit the sick and imprisoned;

- The Naked Jesus I know stands against war and reminds us to love our enemies;

- The Naked Jesus I know calls crazy, shaved head, goatee wearing, tattooed Pastors to his Koinonia.

I get it. None of these statements are norms in our 21st century culture, none of those bring comfort to the hearts of those in the institutional church; I get that. Caring for others more than we care for ourselves is just not in the cards. Come on, we find comfort in the teachings of a Jesus® who tells us "*What is ours, is ours*, and those silly poor people need to just get a job and work for sub-livable minimum wage while staying off Government assistance." Wanting good for others without receiving good in return is foreign to the Jesus® we want to believe in. Telling the rich – the corporations –they are too greedy and must care for others goes against everything our capitalist economic system teaches. Yeah, I get all that – but to be honest, I don't care.

We can all find reasons why we can't do the things the Naked Jesus tells us to do and, believe it or not, I get it. But, if you claim to be a follower of the Naked Jesus, you can't ignore his teachings. Either live by the challenge of his teachings or don't claim to be a follower; it really is that simple. Our 21st century mind wants us to live a life apart from the hurting, broken, and marginalized, in the safety of our homes. We talk about what we should do, but find what we believe are logical reasons why we just can't.

Why? Because we allow our cultural, political, and economic views to distract us from the Naked Jesus, imprison him within the walls of our institutions, and lock the door with the key of fear. When we stand on the diving board and jump, we are freed. We are free to be open (*naked*), but we fear being open. Not because we will meet people we don't know, but because when we are open we are vulnerable and we do not like being vulnerable. Jesus® teaches us vulnerability is dangerous, something that makes us weak, something that causes us to question who we are. Vulnerability is not the *American Way*. While vulnerability is a risk, it is a risk worth taking; it is a risk that can free us. It is the risk that invites us to answer a very important question.

This leads us to our next question, *Who do you say I am?*

CHAPTER SEVEN:
[Who Do You Say I Am?]

 Some time back, I had a very long and interesting,

somewhat intense,

conversation with a pastor

living in the great state of

PROMISE ME YOU'LL ALWAYS REMEMBER: YOU'RE BRAVER THAN YOU BELIEVE. AND STRONGER THAN YOU SEEM. AND SMARTER THAN YOU THINK.
- A. A. Milne

confusion, or what he likes to call

Texas. Toward the end of our

conversation he said, "*I don't like your Jesus.*"

'Hmmmm, really,' I said to myself.

After thinking for a few moments I said, "*You know, I'm not sure I like my Jesus either.*"

At that moment I had an epiphany (*or the rumblings of some bad Mexican food*).

What was my epiphany you ask?

It was this: *If you like the way you see the Naked Jesus 100% of the time, I have to wonder if your Jesus® looks more like you and less like himself.*

You see, the Naked Jesus and his collective narrative should move us, challenge us, change us, and piss us off. When he pisses us off, we should not change the Naked Jesus into the Jesus® we want him to be. If your Jesus® is not pissing you off, I have to wonder why. You see, my Naked Jesus pisses me off on a regular basis. When I was confronted with the question, "Who do you say I am?" let's just say it was a pissing fest.

Here is what I find frustrating about the institutional church –
they don't speak about certain issues, because some clown on
their Leadership Team (usually the one who gives the most
money to the church) decided that certain issues are "political"
and not "spiritual" (*Besides, he wants to feel good when he
leaves the church, so the message has to be a feel good
message*). So, out of fear of losing such a misguided faithful
giver, they will not speak about gun violence because it might
trample on the 2nd Amendment; they don't talk about wealth,
greed and economic inequities because it goes against our
capitalist economic system; they don't speak of privilege
(class, race, or other) because it could offend those deep
pockets they desire to protect; they won't talk about climate
change because their science does not support it. They sell
out the message of the Naked Jesus, so that those who give
are not challenged to view the world differently. They desire

to ignore issues, and the questions that guide our faith journey.

And this births some interesting observations concerning questions, (*wow that seems like a random line*)...

There are some questions we will never know the answer to –

> *Why won't men stop and ask directions?*
> *Why do women open their mouths when they put make-up on?*
> *What was the best thing before sliced bread?*

Other questions we face are somewhat less existential –

> *What will I have for dinner?*
> *Is this shirt clean?*
> *What will I watch on TV?*

While other questions can change our lives forever –

> *Will you marry me?*
> *Should we buy this house?*
> *What will we name our son or daughter?*

However, there is a fourth category of questions: questions whose possibilities you must experience before you can even come close to answering.

Let's kick this party off with one of those questions from the fourth category, a question you will need to experience the possibilities of before you can answer – let me ask the question the Naked Jesus asked his first followers:

Who do you say I am?[74]

Wait, what?

What's that you say?

This is *not* a hard question where I need to experience the possibilities?

---

[74] Matthew 16:15

Are you sure?

It seems hard to me, and there is no way of answering that question without experiencing the teachings of the Naked Jesus first hand. Given that over the past twenty centuries there has been not much those who claim to believe have agreed on, are you sure it's a simple question?

I think it's hard; in fact, I know it is hard because I needed to answer that question myself. But, if you think it is simple, that is because you mistake the first question the Naked Jesus asked "*Who did others tell you I was?*" with the second question the Naked Jesus asked, "*Who do you say I am?*"

Think about it – *no, really, I mean that* – think about that question. Don't reword it; just hold it as it is; let it stand on its own. Think about it from your heart. Don't spew some denominational line, church stance, or an answer someone else said it should be. The answer should come from you, your heart, and your connection to the Divine. You see, the question is directed towards you, for you to answer once you explore the possibilities. The reason I see this as such a hard questions is because, there is no way to answer this question until you experience the Naked Jesus, followed the Naked Jesus, and get to know the Naked Jesus. Answering this question before you follow is dishonest: dishonest to yourself and dishonest to the Naked Jesus.

Give the question some additional thought.

Still think it is a simple question?

When you think about it, it might not be as easy as you assumed. You may have assumed it was easy because you haven't answered the question for yourself. You parroted what others told you, what your church told you, or what your

pastor told you; you didn't answer the question for yourself.
The Naked Jesus wants us to answer the question for
ourselves.

You need to look deep into yourself to find the answer, I had
to. Others cannot tell you what the answer is because it has to
come from you. At best, all they can tell you is who the Naked
Jesus is to them. Even in writing this book, I cannot tell you
what to think or how to answer the question. I can only share
my point of view – you can take it or leave it.

When I answered that question, I needed to get out of that
dark place of corporate, churchy answers full of the noise of
others and find the light I needed to truly, honestly, and
openly follow the teachings of the Naked Jesus. I needed to
rid myself of the garbage the church and others placed on me
to see the Naked Jesus for who the Naked Jesus was and is. I

needed to ponder the question and be honest in my answer on my own, for myself. This was the hardest question I have ever, ever, had to answer. I had to take that journey and come to a conclusion that was good with my soul, good with my faith journey, and stayed true to the collective narrative. I had to be ready, as you need to be, to stand by my answer no matter what I found. Standing on the diving board, this question motivated me to jump.

In my journey to find the Naked Jesus, I needed to start with that question the Naked Jesus asked his First Followers. It seemed natural to me; it was, *if you will*, a no brainer. I couldn't answer that question when I started to follow, because I didn't know the Naked Jesus, or his collective narrative, but I kept the question in mind as I traveled my faith journey. Eventually I was able to answer the question, but it took participation (follow) on my part.

I tend to think we should all start there. When I read the reactions of the First Followers I see people who started their faith journey by *following* to see who Jesus was, so they could someday come to answer that question themselves. You see, too many people answer that question without knowing anything about the collective narrative or the Naked Jesus.

When we start following with the question in mind, we fill in the blanks (those blank spaces in our current neuronet) to give us an answer that will make us acceptable to those around us. Don't go there – search the answer for yourself.

Our search for the Naked Jesus becomes a journey of faith that opens our hearts and spirit to the possibilities. By being open to the possibilities of the answer of the question, our faith journey could take us in different directions than we expected, but it is a journey we all need to take. When our search comes to life, our ability to answer that question is seen in a new light and our understanding of the Divine is given new words. We are able to see the Naked Jesus with our eyes, and *not* with the eyes of another.

To answer the question, you need to explore the collective narrative for yourself. The Naked Jesus didn't ask this question when he first met his first followers. He waited until they got to know him, saw him in action, and connected his life to theirs, and to each other. But it was a question that was in the back of their minds. For the Naked Jesus, it was a *now that you know me* kind of question. To answer this question in any way (*never mind a right way*) is impossible for those new to seeking out the Naked Jesus. At best, before we follow, all we can answer is, *Who do others say I am*? That is not what the Naked Jesus wants to know, he wants to know what *you* think, not what others told you to think.

In Matthew's recording of the life and ministry of the Naked Jesus he records this very interaction between the Naked Jesus and his first followers concerning those very questions.[75] Matthew has the Naked Jesus begin the dialog by asking the wider question of his first followers, "*What are the people saying about me?*" or "*Who did others tell you I was?*" The First Followers liked this question; it was the easy question (like, *What am I having for diner?*)' that is the question we answer today (the *Who did others tell you I was*, not the dinner question). It is easy to answer, because we did not put skin in the game. Their answers didn't really matter, because it started with others (*what are others telling you?*), the Followers didn't have any personal skin in the game, just like many who claim to know Jesus®, they don't answer the

---

[75] Matthew 16:13-20

question *Who do you say I am?*, they answer the question *Who did others tell you I was?*.

Many who decide to believe in Jesus® answer the question, *Who do others say I am?* Because others told you who Jesus® is, or was, you didn't come to your own understanding, you accepted the words of others, and you didn't put skin in the game. I did, I answered the question based on what others told me, and I needed to get past that point. Sure, the others can *prove* their point by quoting a whole bunch of scripture and helping you say the magic prayer, and this is why so many people leave the church. After a time of believing, they see that the words they hear about the Jesus® and the teachings they read about the Naked Jesus don't match. So, the answer others gave them about Jesus® make no sense to them. At that point it is easier to reject the collective narrative all together as some kind of myth – after all, if those who claim to believe in Jesus® are not really following the Naked Jesus, the collective narratives must be a myth.

Most of us simply hear the words of others about the collective narrative and repeat what others told us. We don't put skin in the game, we parrot the response. We allow others to tell us who Jesus® is, and we buy that answer without question. But if you think about it, when asked the question about what others thought, the First Followers' reply seemed the norm – *John the Baptizer, Elijah, Jeremiah or one of the other profits*. While they were pretty good answers, I have a feeling the Naked Jesus heard their answers as company line. Because, when a group of Priests and Officials asked John[76] who he was, they gave him the same list of options – well, exclusive of the *John the Baptizer* option, of course.

---

[76] John 1:19-22

Now that the Naked Jesus got the easy question out of the way it was time to step-up the game, nail them to the wall, and make them put their skin in the game.

The Naked Jesus turned to them and asked, *Who do YOU say I am?* – OUCH. Now the answer was on whoever spoke first, and they were all silent. The Naked Jesus did not direct the question at anyone in particular; it was open to each person to speak out and answer.

Peter spoke up. While I believe they all had an idea of who the Naked Jesus was to them, they didn't want to voice an opinion, they didn't want to put skin in the game. I see this lack of response a few ways. Either the others all agreed with what Peter had to say so there was no reason to say anything else; or the author of Matthew didn't like their responses so he didn't record them; or the others' replies were lost to oral tradition. Whatever the reason, we only get Peter's answer

and, believe it or not, it doesn't matter. What matters is that

Peter put skin deeply into the game when he replied, "*You are

the Christ, the Messiah, the Son of the Living God.*"

For many, that's all they need to know – game over. The

Naked Jesus asked the question, Peter answered, so they

parrot Peter. But the Naked Jesus' response to Peter's answer

is rather interesting and opens up a deeper conversation. The

Naked Jesus did not jump-up, tapping the end of his nose with

his finger shouting, '*ding, ding, ding, Peter you win the prize.*'

The Naked Jesus simply expressed Peter could not have

gotten his answer from any book, or from any teacher. Peter

could only answer that question with the help of the Divine

and by following the Naked Jesus. I find that to be a telling

response to Peter's answer. It tells me the only way for us to

know the answer is to follow the teachings of the Naked Jesus and be open to the Divine's movement in our lives. The response from the Naked Jesus opens up a handful of questions: Does the Naked Jesus mean Peter got his answer directly from the Divine based on his interaction with the Naked Jesus? Could this mean that when we are searching for the Naked Jesus we will not get the answer before we decide to follow? Does it mean we will not get to know the Naked Jesus from reading, from the teachings of a Pastor, or from who others tell us he is? Does the Naked Jesus' reply mean that if we do read the collective narrative to find out who the Naked Jesus is, we need to come to it ourselves without the dogma placed upon us by any institutional religion? Does this mean we need to have skin in the game to actively follow the Naked Jesus? Does this mean we need to follow before we believe?

Our answers just might disrupt the Jesus® of the institutional church who says *Believe before you follow*.

But changing the question, to get the answers they desire, the institutional church seldom (if ever) puts skin in the game. On the website *whoisjesus.com*, they write, "*When the question is personalized, it becomes the most important question one will ever be asked to answer. Who is Jesus to YOU?*"[77] When I read that, my first reaction was, 'Sure, because it is important who Jesus is to me.' After further thought, I realized this is a very bad question. Why? Because the Naked Jesus did not ask *Who am I to you?* The Naked Jesus asked, *Who do you say I am?* These are two different questions.

When we ask the question *Who is Jesus to you?* we get some pretty crazy answers. If we believe (and I do) the Naked Jesus

---

[77] http://www.whoisjesus.com/whois.html - Accessed 2/21/14

was an actual person – an actual living, breathing person – and not a cultural construct of the times, then who are we to change his words to meet our needs? Our needs are met by his words.

When we change his words, we redefine the collective narrative of the Naked Jesus into a Jesus® who meets our wants and not our needs. The question the site asks centers on *you* – the question the Naked Jesus asks centers on *him*.

When I hear people ask the question, *Who is Jesus to you?* My twisted little mind quickly travels to the Will Ferrell/Adam McKay move *Talladega Nights: The Ballad of Ricky Bobby*. If you saw that movie (*If you have not, you so must*) I am certain you remember the dinner scene where Ricky Bobby, his smoking hot wife (*94 on a scale of 100*), and his family gather around the dinner table for a well-balanced meal of fast

food and junk for dinner. Ricky Bobby starts the meal with
grace to the baby Jesus. Soon, Ricky Bobby breaks into a
diatribe after his wife (the smoking hot one) interrupts his
grace to the "sweet baby Jesus."

During grace, his wife (*smoking hot*) told him the baby Jesus
grew-up and was a grown man and not a baby. Ricky Bobby
replies that he knew Jesus was an adult, but liked envisioning
Jesus as a baby (*the sweet little 8lbs 6oz baby Jesus*). That is
the way with so many of us. We love the baby Jesus® but the
adult Naked Jesus drives us crazy, so we take the Naked Jesus
and change him into the baby Jesus® we need him to be – as
it was with Ricky Bobby and his family.

Soon, the conversation turns to answering the question, *Who
is Jesus to me*? (Who is Jesus to you?)

As the possibilities made their way around the table, Jesus was…

A Ninja
A Mischievous Badger
The Lead Singer of Lynyrd Skynyrd (*with large eagle wings*)
Someone in a tuxedo t-shirt (*because it says 'I want to be formal, but I am here to party'*)
A Figure Skater who wears a white outfit and does an interpretive ice dance of my life's journey

Each is a response (*albeit a very funny response*) to what they, as individuals, want Jesus® to be, not who the Naked Jesus is, and none of the responses call us to action.

As I started my faith journey I answered the question, "*Who did others say Jesus was?*" I soon found myself disenchanted with the answer and that is what I see in others who answered the same question the same way I did.

Over time I agonized over the question, *Who do you say I am*? I worked hard to reject the questions, *Who is Jesus to me?*, *Who is the Jesus I desire?*, and *Who is the Jesus others told you about?* I wanted to – no needed to – leave behind the Jesus® others told me about and explore the Naked Jesus. I didn't want to find the Jesus® of my mind or the Jesus® made in the minds of others. I needed to see the Naked Jesus. The Naked Jesus never tells us to *share Jesus* ®with others; he wants us to share the message of hope, of love, of grace, of forgiveness. We share the collective narrative, knowing that who the Naked Jesus is comes later. Answering that question comes later. You begin your process when someone tells you there's hope. Then you show up. Then you admit (*to yourself, mostly*) your need for help; your need for that hope. It is at that point in your faith journey you start understanding there's some sort of Divine power involved, but not worrying about who or what that power is. Your faith journey may take months or years and only after you've seen the fruits of mutual faithfulness and have walked the hard roads together do you start to answer the "Who do you say that I am?" question.

When I found the Naked Jesus, I wanted to follow. I wanted to learn to love others deeply; I wanted to live in grace and forgiveness. I saw what happens when I love others where they are and not where I want them to be. I decided to do more than believe. I decided to follow.

Who do you say I am?

The question focuses our faith walk, not because it gives us a destination but because it gives us a direction. The question leads us to answer with an honest search of our individual spirits in connection to the Divine. Our answer to this question determines our journey and how we interact with others along that path. If we start our faith journey proclaiming *Jesus as our Lord and Savior* before we know him by following him, we misunderstand the connection to the communal. Many tell us to believe then follow; the Naked Jesus tells us follow then believe.

It is important, I believe, that we start our journey without a preconceived idea of who the Naked Jesus is *(or is not)*. We need to be open to disappointment and we need to be open to excitement. Either way, we need to be open. If we start to place our own desires and the teachings of others above those of the Divine, we quickly lose sight of our path. How we answer the question changes us and moves us along an amazing journey of faith, truth, knowledge, and grace. It is perfectly acceptable to enter a Community of Faith and answer the question with "*I have no idea*" or "*Hell if I know.*"

Keep in mind, as we journey into this question, we might not like what we find. What we find could change us deeply and many of us are uncomfortable with change. But that is what the Naked Jesus wants from us: willingness to take the journey, openness to changed hearts and lives, and readiness for revolutionary change. When we open our lives to the possibilities, we realize the revolutionary teachings that can change our lives.

CHAPTER EIGHT:
[Are you tired of this Radical Jesus?]

I am so tired of hearing about this "Radical Jesus®." Aren't you?

Let's face it; most of us grew up with deep distrust of any institutionalized organization. At some point in times-past, this distrust might have been seen as radical, but today, not so much.

> **YOU MUST BE THE CHANGE YOU WISH TO SEE IN THE WORLD.**
> - Mahatma Gandhi

Speaking out against our institutions – e.g., church, government, economic system, and police – is no longer considered an act of radicalism. In fact, radicalization has become so much the social norm we are even ready, willing, and able to question the basic functions of religious groups;

175 | P a g e

this, in my mind, is a good thing – heck, if being radical was such a bad thing do you honestly think advertisers would be using it to sell us products?

Today, we see religious leaders selling out the collective narrative for personal gain, buying multi-million dollar homes, pumping up book sales, and receiving incomes large enough to fund midsize homeless shelters. We see religious leaders and the institutional church wanting more and more and demanding more and more, while all the time believing they're worth it, while claiming a *radical Jesus®*.[78]

It never fails. Whenever I read about this radical Jesus®, or radical leaders, or radical churches, or radical anything, I'm not impressed; I get a little queasy and want to hurl. None of them are even close to radical. I mean really, enough is

---

[78] For some shocking info on this head over to *pimppreacher.com*

enough. OK, ok, I get it. You wear blue jeans to church on Sunday, you have a small tat on your arm (*probably the Jewish name of Jesus you got while you were thinking about how cool it would be for a pastor to have a tat*), a gold or silver stud earring (*in the left ear, because if you wear it in the right ear that would mean you were gay*), a close cropped goatee, and some kind of product in your hair that gives you the *bed-head look*. Big flippin' deal! Heck, you might even use words like *crap* in a sermon every now and then. Here's a shocker for you: none of that makes you a radical. Type in the words "Radical Jesus" in Google and you know what you get? About 27,100,000 results (0.59 seconds).[79] With that many results, there is nothing radical about it.

All the talk, all the books, all the articles, all the sermons concerning the radical nature of Jesus® have zero meaning if

---

[79] Search done on 4/28/14

the radical nature of Jesus® is that you use hip words every now and then and, on top of all that, tell me how your radical Jesus® is while making your radical Jesus® conform to your denominational or personal paradigm. You lost me. There is no way you can convince me you are a *radical anything* when you are just going with the flow and turning radical into conformity. To see the Naked Jesus as a "conformist" is to see the Jesus® the institutional church created, a Jesus® who would *"(of a person) behave according to socially acceptable conventions or standards; be similar in form or type; agree; comply with rules, standards, or laws."* The Naked Jesus was not a conformist at any level. The word "conform" comes from the Middle English meaning *to make like others* – and that is not what the Naked Jesus was about.

If you accept our cultural structures concerning the poor, the broken, the needy, the excluded, you are not even close to being radical.

I'm always surprised when people come to the mystical, magical realization that the Naked Jesus is some kind of radical. *Please, give me a break*. Like people haven't talked about how radical Jesus is for centuries, yet *nothing truly radical comes from it*. We still exclude. We still believe the poor are leeches. We still don't care for the hurting. We still ignore the plight of the marginalized in our culture. We still exclude many from our gatherings. Worse, we fit Jesus® into our political point of view and claim he is radical. And you claim a radical Jesus®? When you tell me how radical your Jesus® is without a faith that is radical in bringing in the excluded, all you're talking is crap (*see, using the word crap, makes me radical*). If you put the word *Radical* in the title of a book all you are looking to do is sell books.[80] If you're going to put the word radical in the title of your book, live up to radical expectations. Stand by it. Own it. Show me your radical Jesus® accepts women as equals and stands behind women's health issues. Show me your radical Jesus® stands for equality in marriage and stands with our Gay and Lesbian brothers and sister. Show me your radical Jesus® started a revolution, not of military power, but in the hearts and minds of all people. Tell me with your actions, not with your words. Don't tell me we have to do all this in the confines of your denominational system or status quo.

I am burned out on people calling the Naked Jesus a radical. The term is so over used it has no value; it's a joke. So, I decided to find a replacement for the word *radical*, but none seemed to fit.

---

[80] I'll be honest, the same can be said about the word "Naked" – I get that.

Basic

Rooted

Essential

Ingrained

Extreme

Fanatic

None of those words do it for me. How about you?

Yeah, those options don't *tingle* my spine either.

You got anything?

Do you have any suggestions?

Here is what I came up with after deep thought and a few beers – and a big bowl of nachos. The Naked Jesus is not a radical; the Naked Jesus is a *revolutionary*. Yeah, that works for me. I get that.

What? What's that you say?

Using the term *revolutionary* doesn't do it for you. Really? Why not?

A *revolutionary* is a person characterized by the nature of a revolution, someone who seeks the sudden and complete change of the existing system. A revolutionary is not someone who fights from inside the system but stands on the outside proclaiming the need for change. Revolutionaries are innovative thinkers who do all their work outside the established system. They just don't fit the norm. The more I think about it, the more I like the word. It fits.

Being a Revolutionary means you need some revolutionary ideas — Oh, yeah — the Naked Jesus had some pretty wild ones.

CHAPTER NINE:
[How about some Revolution with those eggs?]

 Do you want to see jaws drop and eyes twitch in the institutional church? Tell them about the Naked Jesus and his revolutionary teachings on economics and acceptance. That will put a knot in their panties (*mixed metaphor*). Tell them how the Naked Jesus felt about

ALL GREAT TRUTHS BEGIN AS BLASPHEMIES.
George Bernard Shaw

the rich and about redistribution of wealth. Their hearts will stop and they will misquote the collective narrative all over the place as they try to tap-dance around the issue – they may even quote Benjamin Franklyn and claim it's the collective narrative.

The Naked Jesus had some pretty revolutionary ideas about the relationship between the rich and the poor. As I had mentioned earlier, the Naked Jesus had a front row seat to watch how the rich and powerful treated the poor – and to say he had issues with it, seems a mild understatement.

He understood the conditions under which the poor lived, worked, and died – he lived, worked and died under those conditions. The Naked Jesus saw through the power relationship of the rich and poor and deemed it unjust. I imagine a world where this gifted storyteller opens the hearts of those taking advantage of the poor by planting a seed of love and grace; by transforming them into people who see themselves no different than the poor, leading them to share all they have with the whole community in revolutionary ways; but soon, his teaching became polluted by the cultural needs of the rich.

For centuries, the Hebrew people lived under was a system based on the Torah. In the Torah, Leviticus to be particular,[81] a great deal is written about property and how the poor are to be treated. According to Leviticus, all land and wealth belonged to the Divine; people simply held it for a while – there was no "ownership" as we have it today. The Torah broke down time into seven-year periods. At the end of a seven year period they held a Jubilee Year and after a series of seven seven-year blocks (49 years) there was a Sabbatical Year. During the Sabbatical Year, all land was returned to the control of the Priests, who would in turn redistribute the land to new owners.

WHAT?

---

[81] Leviticus chapters 17-26

That's right, all the land was redistributed, but there's more.

All debts were forgiven and all servants were set free.

Evangelicals debate how many of these passages from

Leviticus can be applicable today (*you got it, not many at all*),

since the priesthood and animal sacrifice ended in AD 70.

They ignore the parts they do not like and they embrace other

parts; they ignore the reality that the Naked Jesus taught on

the subject. Normally, they ignore the parts that call for a

redistribution of wealth, but embrace the parts dealing with

sexual relationships and tattoos.

In the time of the Naked Jesus, things changed. The system

that served the Hebrew people so well for centuries shifted to

a system controlled by Roman rule, political arrangements,

power plays and the religious elite. The base of their system

shifted from the Sabbatical Year to control and greed. The

Naked Jesus saw this and his very first proclamation to the

Jewish people centered on those changes. Luke shares in his

writings the Naked Jesus standing in the temple reading from

the book of Isaiah:

> *"God's Spirit is on me; he's chosen me to*
> *preach the Message of good news to the*
> *poor, Sent me to announce pardon to*
> *prisoners and recovery of sight to the blind,*
> *To set the burdened and battered free, to*
> *announce, "This is God's year to act!"*[82]

When the Naked Jesus proclaimed "*This is God's year to act*"

he was saying '*It is time to return to a Sabbatical Year.*'

Everyone who heard his voice that day knew what he was

saying. He was saying Israel had gone too long without a

Sabbatical Year and now was the time. The Naked Jesus was

saying it was time for a revolutionary redistribution of wealth

to the benefit of the poor. It was time for the rich to cut loose

their control and get ready for something new. We don't like

---

[82] Luke 4: 14 – 21

hearing this because those in power would lose that power; it would put our capitalistic system on its head.

Those in power – the religious elite, the rich, the landowners – judged the Sabbatical Year impractical (*go figure*) – pretty much how politicians and those in control of the wealth would see it today. Was this Sabbatical Year really impracticable or was this an excuse to say *nothing will change*? I mean, who wants to give up everything they own and others worked for only to see it given to those useless poor people?

While the Priests knew the Torah, they also knew they were being made rich under the current system. They were part of the elite, so they had no real motive to enforce the Torah, much like many Pastors today would never think about preaching on giving up wealth because that would put a hole in the offering. One Episcopal Priest told me if he preached a message like that he would either be fired or simply have a church filled with poor people – but this idea of greed controlling the ideas expressed in the institutional church was one of the reasons I moved away from being tagged a *Christian*.

Those in the institutional church tend to see only what they desire to see. They see what benefits them and not others. Our cultural value of greed motivates many to hold fast to what they believe they own. Even though they teach that everything belongs to the Divine, they don't believe it. Usually, when the institutional church teaches that everything belongs to the Divine, it means they want to increase giving. Many proclaim to be followers of the Naked Jesus while holding fast to the teachings of Ayn Rand.[83]

They value those who make billions while the poor are seen as *useless takers* taking what they didn't earn out of *our* hard earned money. Wealth is something the rich created, something they have the ultimate right (and only right) to control. It is theirs and they have no desire to share. This *its mine, not yours* perception imprisons us and limits our connection to the collective narrative. The Naked Jesus knew this was wrong. He knew the work of regular people is the center of any earthly economic system and an imbalance between the rich and poor would destroy – and is destroying – the world.[84]

---

[83] She was the founder of the "Objectivist movement" -
http://en.wikipedia.org/wiki/Objectivist_movement
[84] http://tinyurl.com/onm45ug

The problems facing our world are not found in some evil force, no matter what you name it. The evils of our world are found in human greed: the greed to control wealth, the greed to control food supplies, the greed to control natural resources, the greed to control everything. Consumer based theology – institutional theology – tells us we can do what we desire to this planet and treat people as we desire because we are forgiven. I have actually heard Pastors teach that we can mess this planet up because Jesus® is returning and all will be fine; Jesus® will make everything right again. If we are truly honest with ourselves we need to admit that we are the cause of the problems. To assume the Divine will fix the problems we face is a very poor theological stance.

When a rich man (*a man of greed*) approached the Naked Jesus and asked how he could receive eternal life, the Naked Jesus replied, "*Go sell your possessions; give everything to the poor. All your wealth will then be in heaven. Then come follow me."*[85] Needless to say, the rich man was not overly excited with that answer. In fact, he was downright bummed by it – so much so, he just left. The Naked Jesus then looked at his first follower and added,

> "*Do you have any idea how difficult it is for the rich to enter God's kingdom? Let me tell you, it's easier to gallop a camel through a needle's eye than for the rich to enter God's kingdom."*

The interesting part, is the line "*it's easier to gallop a camel through a needle's eye than for the rich to enter God's kingdom"* because, as we talked about before, the Naked Jesus tells us that the Kingdom of the Divine is all around us. If that is the case, and I believe it is, the Naked Jesus is telling us the greedy rich are disconnected from the world around them; they cannot see the Divine's Kingdom because they are

---

[85] Matthew 19:21

centered on, and blinded by, their wealth. The story of the rich man and Lazarus echoes this theme that wealth is of no value.[86] The Naked Jesus opens this story:

> "*There once was a rich man, expensively dressed in the latest fashions, wasting his days in conspicuous consumption. A poor man named Lazarus, covered with sores, had been dumped on his doorstep. All he lived for was to get a meal from scraps off the rich man's table. His best friends were the dogs who came and licked his sores.*"

No matter who you are, wealth controls us; it blinds us to the needs of others. When we hold fast to wealth, or the idea of wealth, we lose ourselves to the idea of helping others. We see our needs, even our scraps, as ours and we do not need to share anything.

---

[86] Luke 16:19-31

With these stories in mind, we need to ask ourselves some questions and answer them in context of the controlling nature of wealth.

Does wealth separate us from the Divine?
Are we called to share our wealth with those in need?
Does wealth create an *us vs. them* reality?
Is wealth, in and of itself, wrong?

Now, not all people of wealth are people of greed. Some give a great deal to those in need. But to be honest with you, if a person is worth $65 billion dollars, and they give away one billion, it's like an average person who has $100.00, giving another $1.50 – what we give should be seen in relationship to what we are worth – besides, we need to ask ourselves, *Do we honestly need $65 billion?*

The Naked Jesus, as a revolutionary, saw the need for change and fought the system to ensure an equal distribution of wealth. He deemed the power relationship between the rich

and the poor unjust. We need to do the same. We need to be

willing to stand before a CEO making some 1,750 times what

the average worker in the same company makes and calls it

unjust.[87] We need to stand before the banker receiving

millions in bonuses and call it unjust. We need to question the

banks holding empty houses in hopes of a market uptick while

many are left homeless and ask why.[88] We need to stand

before the corporations who hold the interests of the

stockholders over the workers and consumers and we need

take action. We need to demand people be paid a livable

wage.

The rich and powerful don't like notions of redistribution of

wealth. They claim such ideas are communist or socialist. Not

---

[87] http://tinyurl.com/p6d3oj2: Accessed 1/27/2014
[88] http://tinyurl.com/cyhx3fn: Accessed on 1/27/2014

me. This is the teaching of the Naked Jesus. Our walk, our call, is to help those in need and stand up to any system that serves to control them. We need to stand on the teachings of the Naked Jesus and stand up for justice.

I know what you're thinking, "*The poor will be with us always*" right?

If one more person take the phrase "The poor you will always have with you"[89] out of context (which is always just an excuse to avoid asking the hard questions about the poor and poverty), I'm going to tear my hair out (ok, first I'll have to stop shaving my head). I have heard this statement used countless times as the Naked Jesus' prediction of the state of poverty. People take it to mean that the poor will always, and forever, be with us so don't worry about trying to eliminate

---

[89] Matthew 26:11

poverty, because we can't. Poverty is clearly God's will. Jesus® said so, right? *NO HE DID NOT.* Read the rest of the verse, "*but you will not always have me.*" The Naked Jesus is not telling them not to worry about poverty because there is nothing they could do about it. What he is saying is he himself is not going to be around much longer. The Naked Jesus is not making a statement of fact; he is making a statement of comparison.

But how do we do this?

How do we openly express our stand against greed in favor of the poor?

How do we openly stand against the culture?

We take the next step toward revolution by openly inviting and loving those in need.

Welcoming people into your faith community is not revolutionary. Affirming the life of another is not revolutionary. Think about it. Most churches that claim to be *welcoming* or *affirming* are not very welcoming or affirming. Sure, they are welcoming if you are like those currently in the church, but not if you are different. Many in the institutional church will protest, because they can point to one or two people in their church who are poor, and "we let them in." But I wonder if being "welcoming and affirming' is something good?

My friend (and Editor) Caedmon Michael puts it this way,

> "I'm just realizing the irony of 'welcoming and affirming.' It is, at face, an act of a privileged group offering to an oppressed group the 'opportunity' to enter into the privileged world, to come and be part of the privileged group's culture. The oppressed members are allowed to maintain the distinctions of their oppression, but are

otherwise expected to be assimilated into the privileged culture. This is not justice."[90]

While we will get more into this later in this book, just realize people don't want to be welcomed or affirmed — they want to be *wanted*. WANTING others *is* revolutionary.

The **Naked** Jesus; A Journey Out of Christianity and Into Christ

CHAPTER TEN:
[Are We There Yet?]

 One of the greatest freedoms I have experienced in my walk with the Divine was realizing my life is in process. Come to think of it, your life is in process, we are all in process. If we deny our lives are in process, we are only fooling ourselves. Each day I learn something new. I develop some new expression of my faith. I

> SIR. MY CONCERN IS NOT WHETHER GOD IS ON OUR SIDE MY GREATEST CONCERN IS TO BE ON GOD S SIDE. FOR GOD IS ALWAYS RIGHT.
> - Abraham Lincoln

see something new to add to my faith journey. None of us are defined by any predetermined destination but by the intertwining of our lives with others and with the Divine, which is our faith journey. In other words, it is not the destination that matters, but how we enjoy the journey.

When my daughter was growing-up she would ask that one question designed to drive most traveling parents crazy, "*Are we there yet?*"

We never got mad at her when she asked that question. Instead, we quickly learned to turn the trip into a game. We would find towns with weird names and make up stories of how they got that name – some of the stories were just too funny. Shellene and I play the same game when we travel.

Making the trip fun and turning what can be (and often is) something very boring into something exciting took her mind off the destination and focused it on the journey. We made the journey fun and the destination took second place to the trip.

When we grasp the revolutionary nature of the Naked Jesus we need to have that same experience with our faith journeys.

When we redefine our neuronet we don't focus on is the destination (*heaven or hell*) because when we do we miss the opportunity to make the journey of life fun and meaningful. Besides, following the teachings of the Naked Jesus doesn't produce a prize or punishment at the end. If we set our eyes on the prize (*or punishment*), we're not following. We spend our time looking to the undefined future and not enough on our surroundings — we miss the opportunity to help others because we are centered on our own ending, our own needs. On a metaphysical level, asking the question "Are we there yet?" seems silly because at some level we are already there — we are always somewhere.

Throughout my faith journey, I have been torn between the concepts the institutional church shared and what I read in scripture. I struggled with many of the concepts for years; and the closer I walked with the Naked Jesus the closer I came to realizing much of what the institutional church taught was wrong. I have had many debates with myself concerning the meanings of the concepts in relationship to what the Naked Jesus said and did and to how the church understands them. The only time I didn't like debating myself over these issues was when I felt I was losing the argument, which happened more times than I am willing to admit.

I needed to take my faith journey in a new direction, remap my neuronet. Much of what I read from collective narrative didn't connect with the claims of truth I heard in the institutional church. Turning our faith journey was, and still is, confusing when our eyes are set on the destination, not the journey.

People who speak against the *core doctrines* of the institutional church are pushed aside or insulted. Calling any part of the institutional church stance into question

automatically places you outside the norm, accused of not

being a true believer. This is a poor place to start any process

of understanding the Naked Jesus. We are not asking

questions seeking to deconstruct our faith. We are asking to

rediscover the meaning of the collective narrative in

relationship to the Naked Jesus. We want to recapture what

the Naked Jesus wants from us. Let me share a few of my

discoveries.

Generally speaking (*I hate speaking for any group*),

those of us who accept the label *Liberal* or *Progressive*

do have a solid understanding of sin, salvation and

morality. What we don't have is an arbitrary

determination of what is or is not divinely revealed

through the collective narrative.

Just mentioning the word *SIN*[91] can quickly turn any peaceful conversation into a debate where each group holds their definition of sin as *the true, right, and biblical truth*. While having differences is not an issue, it becomes an issue when one group insists they're right and everyone else is wrong and falls outside the definition of a *True Christian*. For such a small word, *sin* is packed with some pretty powerful emotions and some pretty powerful judgments.

So, what is sin?

The collective narrative describes sin as *the breaking, or transgression, of God's Commands,*[92] but what does this mean? What commands are we breaking, or transgressing, in order to be sinning? We have to ask

---

[91] Hamartiology is the branch of theology that deals with *the study of sin*
[92] 1 John 3:4

ourselves, when the Naked Jesus was talking about breaking any of the commandments, was he speaking of the some 613 commandments[93] found in Judaism? Can we say that the Naked Jesus was talking about the Hebrew commands as he knew them when he spoke about sin? When the Naked Jesus tells people *to go and sin no more*, what is he talking about?

Really, what IS sin?

To understand sin, we must start with admitting the basic origin of sin is unclear. According to the institutional church, *sin* came into this world through the interaction of Adam and Eve[94] with a snake[95] in

---

[93] For a complete list of these laws, check out this site: http://tinyurl.com/nhbw333

[94] Genesis 3. In Paul's letter to the Romans (5:12) he says "sin came into this world from one man" – but he never says who that man is – a

some *mythical* garden.[96] They call this interaction

original sin or *The Fall of Humanity*.

Interestingly enough, the term *original sin* isn't found

anywhere in the collective narrative. In fact, Judaism

has no concept of original sin and remember the

Naked Jesus was a Jew. If we think about it, we have

to ask which understanding would the Naked Jesus

have held: original sin or not?

Keep in mind, Augustine (354-430) was the first

theologian to teach that humanity was born into this

world in a state of sin. Judaism believes and teaches

Christological reading of Paul's letter places Adam in the shadow of the "One Man."

[95] The serpent is seen as "Satan" – but the collective narrative simply calls the serpent a serpent and never implies the serpent is anything else.

[96] The story of Adam and Eve is not a literal story. It is a mythical story trying to explain how the Divine created humanity that should not be taken word for word.

that humanity enters the world free of sin, with a soul that is pure and innocent and untainted. So, it is natural to assume that the Naked Jesus never thought of original sin, so he had to be thinking of something else.

In Matthew's writing in the collective narrative, the Naked Jesus tells us to "*live generously and graciously towards one another, the way God lives towards you.*"[97] Reading those words started me on this journey of processing my understanding of sin. Maybe, just maybe, sin is not that we transgress against the Divine, but – maybe, just maybe – it is that we transgress against each other.

---

[97] Matthew 5:48

In the context of living a generous and gracious life,

sin (*for lack of a better word at this time*) *is our*

transgressions against each other; it is found in the

way we treat each other in our daily lives – it is our

focus on the destination and not the journey. This is

echoed when Matthew adds the story of the sheep and

goats.[98] In this part of the collective narrative, the

Naked Jesus shares that when we feed the hungry,

give drink to the thirsty, house the homeless, clothe

the cold, care for those who are sick, and visit those in

need of our touch, we are doing what the Divine

desires of us. If we ignore the plight of others, we

violate the Divine's call for us to care for others. You

see, we are called to hold humanity in trust. When we

violate this call to care we are transgressing against

---

[98] Matthew 25:31-46

our care for the hurting, the broken, and the marginalized and in turn you violate the person. In that, you sin. One could say that we sin against the Divine by proxy because we are all created in the image of the Divine. For the Naked Jesus, sin is not how you dress, who you love, how you look, or how we interact with the Divine – it is when we are abusive to others and ignore their needs, and place our needs over theirs.

It's how we treat the poor, how we treat those in need, how we treat the hurting, how we treat the broken, and how we treat the excluded, which includes how we treat our gay and lesbian brothers and sisters, it is the harmful words we use to bring others down. Sin is defined by how we treat, or ignore, those rejected by the institutional church and society. Sin is found in our ignoring and disregarding them; we are in fact abusing them. Sin is where we do not open our hearts, our wallets, our time, and our lives to those in need of our love. Sin is when we meet someone for the first time and wonder *what can this person do for me*? A generous and gracious life means that when we meet people for the first time, we ask ourselves *what can I do for them*?

According to the classic evangelical theology, to become a *true servant of God* we must admit we are sinners. However, this is not an idea that flows easy from the collective narrative. To admit that we transgress against another seems silly, because the Divine already knows we transgress. The Naked Jesus does not tell us to admit we transgress, but to admit our transgressions, meaning we need to be in relationship with those we transgressed against.

The evangelical[99] call to arms is to *ADMIT, COMMIT* and *SUBMIT*[100] *(with some adding, TRANSMIT[101]): Admit* you are a sinner, *Commit* to the teachings of the church (*as they see them*), and *Submit* to the authority of the church and its leaders (The "Transmit" part comes in because you have to tell others to do the same thing).

In collective narrative we are called to admit our sins – our transgressions against others (to stand naked before each other) – and seek forgiveness from them and the Divine, but nowhere does the Naked Jesus tell

---

[99] If there is one thing the Institutional church loves, is when words rhyme
[100] http://www.deceptioninthechurch.com/admitcommitsubmit.html: Accessed on 1/27/14
[101] http://tinyurl.com/qgnjspj - Accessed 3/1/14

us to admit we are sinners. James, the brother of the Naked Jesus, tells us to develop a *common practice* and *"Confess your sins to each other and pray for each other so that you can live together whole and healed."*[102] This is hard for many to grasp because we want sin to be something ethereal, not something we do to one another or others do to us, and it is not something we are willing to admit. We do not desire to be accountable for our actions, or lack of action. By telling people that all they need to do is admit they are sinners and not telling them to address their sins, they make it easy to not confront the wrongs done to others and how they treat others – it is, if you will, a cheap form of grace, an imaginary grace.

---

[102] James 5:16-18

Generally speaking, there are two concepts of sin (transgressions) in the collective narrative. The first is *stepping across a boundary or limit* (Historically we have translated the word "*sin*" in the *"Lord's Prayer"* as *Trespass*).[103] Sin is overstepping our place, crossing boundaries of respect, care, grace, love, and concern for others, and seeking good for ourselves at the expense of others; we 'trespass against them.' We believe our needs, desires, and wants exceed the needs, desires, and wants of others. We must have it our way or we reject the relationship. We show many forms of partiality.[104] This concept of sin can be seen as straying off course and continuing in our desired path to the exclusion of others. Standing against

---

[103] Matthew 6:9–13: Sometimes, the word hamartía, is translated as sin or debt

[104] James 2:9 – "But if you show partiality you are committing sin and are convicted by the law as transgressors"

marriage equality or against social justice issues are good examples.

The second concept of sin in the Collective Narrative is *missing the mark*. This is a hunting term where the bow hunter misses the intended target. It is aiming for perfection, but never quite hitting it. Think of it as knowing how you should treat people, but you never quite do it right, which leads us to new questions:

What are the boundaries?
What is the target we are missing?

To the Naked Jesus, the answer to both questions is very simple: *LOVE,* and it's not a Subaru.

Love is the boundary that centers us; it is the target we seek to hit. The Naked Jesus' ministry is saturated in Divine love. From start[105] to finish,[106] the Naked Jesus was marked by the love of the Divine and wanted others to see that love. The boundary set for us is to live in that same love. Humanity was conceived in love[107] and the Naked Jesus desires we live in love – no, it is not that he desires, he commands us to live in love.

Now, we may not like being commanded to do anything – we are always looking for a way out – but the Naked Jesus does command us to love. It's not an option, there is no way out of this – we must love everyone. The Naked Jesus tells us none can call themselves followers of his teachings if they don't live in love and share that love with others. It's not a *well,*

---

[105] Matthew 3:16-17
[106] Luke 23:34-35
[107] Matthew 6:2-4

I love the lovable, but those creepy broken people are just too hard to love,[108] it is an in your face, nailed to the wall, skin in the game, on the mark, *Love Everyone.*

Love the unlovable.[109]
Love your enemies.[110]
Love one another.[111]
Love those creepy broken people.

Love was so important to the Naked Jesus that he said, "*remember the root command: Love one another.*"[112] Think about that. The *root command* is love, which means love feeds us and helps us grow. Love is the foundation of everything. Love boots our operating system (*our new neuronet*) when we follow

[108] Matthew 5:43-47
[109] Matthew 5:43-47
[110] Matthew 5:43-47
[111] John 13:34-35
[112] John 15:17

the teachings of the Naked Jesus. The Naked Jesus is

saying, *live this revolutionary idea of loving everyone.*

Love is the root that holds up the tree of life. Our

operating system should boot with love at its core. But

for many in the institutional church, love is not part of

their root system.[113] For them, love is something

harsh, controlling, and demanding; it is something

shared with those who are like them, those who they

seem as "normal." They speak of excluding others in

some twisted idea called *tough love* that is not even

close to anything found in the collective narrative. It

has always confused me when people in the

institutional church proclaim their love for Jesus®

while at the same time denying that love to others.

Over my lifetime I have known many people in the

---

[113] John 5:41-44

institutional church who told me they loved me, but never showed an ounce of love towards me. But the Naked Jesus tells us, *"If you love me, show it by doing what I've told you."*[114]

As I started to redefine my neuronet on the idea of what the Naked Jesus shares as "sin" my eyes started to open to other possibilities of the story of salvation.

What does it mean to be saved?

In the collective narrative the word *sốzō* is one of the words used for being *saved*. Generally it means to be *made well* or to be *made whole*. Do you remember what James said about sin? *"Confess your sins to each other and pray for each other so that you can live*

---

[114] John 14:15-17

together whole and healed."[115] Notice that James tells us that when we confess our wrong doings, to others (stand naked), we are made "whole" and "healed."

In Matthew's writings we read the story of a woman who suffered for 12 years from hemorrhaging.[116] As the Naked Jesus was walking past the woman she reached out and touched his robe. The Naked Jesus looked at her and said, "*You are made whole.*" What I have always found interesting about this story is that at no time does she ask to be saved, at no point is she required to admit she is a sinner, and at no point is she asked to say a special prayer, yet she is made whole, she is *saved* simply by reaching out to the Naked Jesus.

---

[115] James 5:16-18
[116] Matthew 9:20-22

In some versions of the collective narrative *sōzō* is translated as "saved," but what if we read those passages with *being made whole* instead? What would change?

Let's take three examples from the writings of John. Here is how the three passages appear in the New American Standard Bible (NASB) of the collective narrative:

> *John 3:17* "For God did not send the Son into the world to judge the world, but that the world might be **saved** through Him."
>
> *John 5:34* "But the testimony which I receive is not from man, but I say these things so that you may be **saved**."
>
> *John 10:9*
> "I am the door; if anyone enters through Me, he will be **saved**, and will go in and out and find pasture."

Now, what happens when we change *saved* into *made whole*:

> *John 3:17* "For God did not send the Son into the world to judge the world, but that the world might be **made whole** through Him."

> *John 5:34* "But the testimony which I receive is not from man, but I say these things so that you may be **made whole**."

> *John 10:9*
> "I am the door; if anyone enters through Me, he will be **made whole**, and will go in and out and find pasture."

Being saved, walking in the salvation narrative of the Divine, is being *made whole* in the Divine. Jesus echoes this idea of being whole when he tells his first followers he is leaving them, "*well and whole*."[117] After

---

[117] John 14:25-27

years of following the Naked Jesus' teachings one is made well and whole.

But how does one become whole?
What does being whole mean?

For the Naked Jesus, being made whole is found in our understanding of being *born anew*, or *born from above*.

But what does that mean?

I know what you're thinking: '*OK, now we get to this born again stuff, the tongues, the dancing, the handling of snakes – no thanks*.' This is the point where you close the book screaming – but wait, it is not what you think.

In John's writings he records the Naked Jesus saying:

"*You're not listening. Let me say it again. Unless a person submits to this original creation—the 'wind-hovering-over-the-water' creation, the invisible moving the visible, a baptism into a new life—it's not possible to enter God's kingdom. When you look at a baby, it's just that: a body you can look at and touch. But the person who takes shape within is formed by something you can't see and touch—the Spirit—and becomes a living spirit.*"[118]

As I was processing out of the shallow end of the pool, I started to see this part of the collective narrative as something very different; for me being *Born from Above* (I like that translation better than the *Born Again* translation) means going back to our original creation: who was the *you* the Divine created? Being born from above is not about speaking some special language, or being filled with some alien presence, or

---

[118] John 3:5-6

even handling snakes. It is that we return to our original creation, to who the Divine desired us to be before the world filled us with the bullshit that clouds our thoughts and labels us: you're fat, you're useless, you're ugly, you're stupid, you're a fag, you're a dyke, you're a bitch, you're worthless – just to name a few.

Being born from above is the Divine bringing us back to the person the Divine desired us to be from the very point of our birth. Being born from above is finding happiness in relationship with the Divine, because we are who we are supposed to be, not what the world labeled us. As I mentioned before, the Naked Jesus adds emphasis to this when he says, *"You're blessed when **you're content with just who you are**—no more, no less. That's the moment you find yourselves proud owners of everything that can't* *be bought."*[119] When we are born from above, we accept ourselves, we accept the *us* the Divine created – we accept we are born from above from our original birth, we are made whole.

You find wholeness in finding the *you* the Divine intended you to be; I became whole when I accepted the me the Divine created. In Judaism, salvation is open to everyone and not just a select few. Since the Naked Jesus was a Jew, why would he have a different concept of salvation? Why would he limit the salvation narrative to a select few?

For the first 1,000 years or so of Christendom, there was no doctrine of propitiation[120] and the amazing love the Naked

---

[119] Matthew 5:5

[120] Propitiation is the doctrine that the Divine, through the punishment and death of Jesus, is appeased and conciliates the Divine who would

Jesus shared on the cross was not about atoning for our sins.
I know! Shocking, right? In fact, we find little about the
concept of penal atonement in the writings of the early
Apologists. The early church held closer to the teachings of
Judaism, including that the teaching of sins passing from
father to son went against the Collective Narrative. When we
look at the Hebrew narrative, Deuteronomy[121] and Ezekiel[122]
we read that the son cannot inherit the sins of the father.
(There are a few passages in Exodus[123], Deuteronomy[124], and
Numbers[125] that say the sins of the father will pass to the
second, third and even fourth generations, but this has to do
with how long the sins of the father will last *with the father*
and is a different discussion.) In John's writings, the Naked

---

otherwise be offended by our sin and would demand we pay the penalty
for it.
[121] Deuteronomy 24:16
[122] Ezekiel 18:20
[123] Exodus 20:5 and 34:7
[124] Deuteronomy 5:9
[125] Numbers 14:18

Jesus is confronted by a blind man seeking healing and his disciples ask him if the man was being punished for his sins or the sins of his father and Jesus replies, *"Neither."*[126]

A gracious and generous atonement flies in the face of the institutional church's *in-your-face* doctrine of judgment, paying a price and seeking the ending prize. When we hold to an in-your-face atonement, we lose the *mystery* of the Crucifixion, and in turn we miss the wonder of the Resurrection. We miss the mystery of the Divine working in our times. We need to *find a reason*, ignoring that we may never know a true, lasting reason.

It might have surprised you to hear *Penal Substitution* is a recent development. Penal Substitution theorizes *divine forgiveness* must be satisfied with *divine justice*. That is, the

---

[126] John 9:1-3

Divine is unwilling, or unable, to forgive without first requiring

a satisfaction (*payment*) for the transgression. This seems to

push against everything the Naked Jesus spoke during his life

and ministry. The Naked Jesus forgave the transgressions of

others on a regular basis without any need for payment or

restitution. The Naked Jesus also tells us to forgive others

without receiving payment. If we see the Naked Jesus as the

avatar of the Divine, as the Divine incarnated, as the Christ,

his actions and words must be the words and actions of the

Divine. If the Naked Jesus never spoke about making a

payment, why would the Divine?

It wasn't until Anselm's[127] famous (keep in mind, "famous" is a

relative term) work *Cur Deus Homo*[128] in 1098 that attention

focused on a *paying a price* theology of redemption. Anselm's

---

[127] Anselm of Canterbury (1033 – 21 April 1109)
[128] "Why God Became Human?"

theology centered more on the English Penal Code and less on the collective narrative. Anselm held that if humanity sinned *(transgressed or crossed boundaries)*, the Divine must demand some form of Divine repayment, like wanting a thief to pay the price of an item stolen from you. For Anselm, the Naked Jesus died to pay that price. This idea grew and took root under the reformers during the Reformation five centuries later. But, if we see a gracious and generous atonement we see Jesus' act on the Cross was a triumphant act on the part of the Divine over *the bondage of the world,* freeing us from the abuses we suffer every day; evident by the wondrous act of the Resurrection. Jesus' death showed us the power of the Divine to overcome a hostile world to walk in love, grace and forgiveness. In reading the collective narrative, we see this evident in the life, ministry, death and resurrection of the Naked Jesus. As a result of this act of love, we are freed from the bonds of this world that hold us and we are given a direct connection to a free life in the Divine, no payment needed, to find wholeness of self. With the world pulling us one way, the Divine's actions invite humanity to understand the connection with the Divine is free and based in love and not some kind of *Divine repayment for sins*.

The problem with the institutional church and salvation is that they see it as exclusively for those who believe what they believe. For them, salvation will come after death with eternal life. While the body is pushing up daisies, and the soul is either in the clouds or some cavern in the center of the earth. They transformed *being made whole* into the cosmic distortion of holding a ticket to heaven. Salvation is the golden ticket into the *Willy Wonka* factory of the afterlife.

The institutional church believes *eternal life* only exists after death. But is that the case? Do you only get eternal life after you die? Jesus continually tells us the Kingdom of the Divine is around us and we live in the Kingdom now; we are born into that Kingdom and eternal life starts when we are born, or before, and continues long after we leave this meat-puppet we call a body. This is why returning to the *you* the Divine desired you to be is so very important. In fact, we all need to return to the Divine. We are born into the salvation narrative; we are co-participants with the Divine, and each other, in this world. If we desire, we can opt out at some point, but all are born into the salvation narrative. We are all born into the Kingdom of the Divine; we are all born connected to the Divine.

The past sins of an ancestor did not change that reality one bit.

It is when the world pulls us away and pollutes our thoughts of the *you* the Divine created that we doubt who we are, and *who* we were created to be.

If being saved is *being made whole,* how does salvation now fit into the collective narrative?

The salvation narrative is not only found in what the Naked Jesus did on the Cross. The salvation narrative is found in the Naked Jesus coming so we could have a whole relationship with the Divine and dying so we could see the fullness of the Divine, know the Divine's hope for the world, and live in partnership with the Divine and one other.

Saying the Naked Jesus died for our sins misses the mark (*get the play on words*). It misses the reality of what the Naked Jesus shared and what Judaism teaches. *Substitution* theology does not work. It is a narrative of humanity that does not fit the narrative of hope and love. If the Kingdom of the Divine is now, salvation and eternal life starting after death is weird and out of touch with the collective narrative the Naked Jesus shares concerning the Kingdom of the Divine. If the Kingdom of the Divine is now, we are born into the salvation narrative.

Substitution atonement has made salvation cheap: "*accept Jesus as your Lord and Savior, say this magic prayer, come to church on Sundays, and you can still treat people like crap because you are forgiven.*" This is a twisted view of how the salvation narrative works because it allows people to do as they desire without changed lives under the misguided assumption it does not matter how you treat another because you are simply forgiven. Substitution theology is Jesus® dying for our sins to remove any responsibility we have for living a changed life. I am sure you heard it before – *I'm not perfect, just forgiven* – which really means, *I can treat people like shit, because I am forgiven - all is good.*

As I moved closer to the Naked Jesus I realized a generous salvation comes when we understand our place in partnership with the Divine; when we see our place in the collective narrative; when we live in hope, love, grace, and forgiveness; and when we live with others inside the collective narrative. Salvation comes when we realize we are made whole in the Divine and in that wholeness are open to loving and caring for all people. Salvation comes when we stand against the evils of those who seek only self gratification: greedy CEO's, bankers, politicians – people who claim to be walking with the Divine but miss the teachings of the Divine in many ways. Could this be what Paul means when he write that we need to work out our salvation in fear and trembling?[129]

When we redefine our neuronet to seeing a mindful understanding of sin and salvation, our minds become open to seeing a very different understanding of the Sacraments.

---

[129] Philippians 2:12

CHAPTER ELEVEN:
[How many Sacraments are there?]

 Earlier stages of the church gave us practices that help us step outside our current thinking and see the Divine with new eyes, to see a gracious salvation story. Traditionally, we have called these practices *sacraments*.

A punishment-centered Cross shoves the Divine into a human understanding of judgment which is not the Divine's

> I CAN T GIVE YOU A SURE FIRE FORMULA FOR SUCCESS. BUT I CAN GIVE YOU A FORMULA FOR FAILURE: TRY TO PLEASE EVERYBODY ALL THE TIME.
> Herbert Bayard Swope

understanding of love and nonviolence. It closes our hearts to the real power and grace of the sacraments; we create cheap, meaningless motions some call sacraments, and others call ordinances. We see this in the creation of, what is called,

"*Communion Packets.*"[130] We have made the sacrament of

Communion cheap and easy: when we look at the collective

narrative, we have lost sight of what it means to live a

sacramental life in the Naked Jesus.

When I was in seminary, one of my professors told us a

sacrament was "*something Jesus® did and something he told

us to do.*" He added, *"to be a sacrament, it needed both

elements.*" While the *official* definition of a sacrament is, *"a

religious ceremony or act of the Christian Church that is

regarded as an outward and visible sign of inward and spiritual

divine grace,*" I have always found my professor's definition a

bit more workable.

---

[130] http://www.amazon.com/Celebration-Individual-Communion-Wafer-Juice/dp/B007502IPY accessed 4/28/14

He went on to explain that, as Protestants, we have only *two* sacraments. Because Jesus® was baptized and was baptizing (even though others did the baptizing), baptism is a sacrament. Because Jesus® took communion and told us to take communion, communion is a sacrament. This idea that *if Jesus® did it and told us to do it, we should do it* stuck with me.

Over my years in ministry I have seen a sacrament as just that – *The Naked Jesus did it and he told us to do it*. Pretty simple, right? Yes. And no. You see, this definition got me thinking. If a sacrament is something the Naked Jesus did and told us to do, we have more than two sacraments; we just don't want to admit we do.

If a sacrament is something the Naked Jesus did and told us to do, the sacraments are open to ideas like love, forgiveness, and caring for the poor. The Naked Jesus did them and told us to do them, opening up so much about church and what we should be doing in relationship to how we live. Even if we take the "official definition" of *act of the Christian Church that is regarded as an outward and visible sign of inward and spiritual divine grace*, we can still see them as sacraments, because they are "acts of the Christian Church" – or should be.

This view of the sacraments opens us to some amazing possibilities. Every time – without exception – we meet new people, we must start the process of falling in love with them. It doesn't matter who they are, what others think about them, or what they have (*or have not*) done in their lives. By falling in love with them we invite them into our hearts, into our lives, and are open to them inviting us into their hearts and lives. Even if they don't invite us into their lives, it doesn't remove our call to fall in love with them, to extend ourselves –

push ourselves if you will – beyond our comfort zone so we can invite others into our lives.

Here are some sacraments to share with the church:

Love is a sacrament.

Caring for the poor is a sacrament.

Caring for the broken is a sacrament.

Caring for the unclean is a sacrament.

Welcoming the excluded is a sacrament.

Forgiveness is a sacrament.

Can you think of more?

When I expanded my views of a sacrament, I opened myself up to many possibilities. It moved me past a stagnation point and develops a pivot point in me, allowing me to move in exciting new directions; realizing that "we are not there yet."

The sacraments move us to challenge the dichotomy of secular and sacred and cause us to embrace the truth that all people are sacred. They move us to develop a new and different theology of the church, a theology of a community of faith.

CHAPTER TWELVE:
[What Would Happen If We Thought In Terms Of Koinology?]

I wanted to end this book with an idea that kind of wrapped everything up with a pretty little bow, but to be honest with you, I can't. I suck at wrapping gifts. But I did want to share something I am in process with and invite you to take it and run with it. If we see things differently, if we see new sacraments, different ways of understanding the salvation story, and different way of connecting to others and the Divine, we need to see the "*theology of the church*" in a very different light, we need to have a "*theology of a community of faith.*"

> THE COMMUNITY STAGNATES WITHOUT THE IMPULSE OF THE INDIVIDUAL. THE IMPULSE DIES AWAY WITHOUT THE SYMPATHY OF THE COMMUNITY.
> - William James

Have you ever heard the term *Ecclesiology?*

If you're like me, all those *ologies* get confusing; most ologies drive me crazy. I always get *Ecclesiology* mixed-up with *Eschatology* – in my limited little brain they sound alike. To separate them, I need a dictionary or cheat sheet.

For those who know the difference, let me just say…relax, this chapter has nothing to do with Eschatology. But I do want to talk a bit about Ecclesiology.

Ecclesiology is the theological study of the church. In recent years it has come to mean how one deals with the nature, constitution, and function of the church. I was once told Ecclesiology helps us understand the role *of* the church and our role *in* the church. I'm told it asks the following questions:

What is the Church?
What is the relationship between a believer and the Church?

What is the authority of the Church?
What does the Church do?
What structure should the Church have?

Like I do with the word *Christian* I have several real problems

with the word *church*. The least of which is that the word

church doesn't appear in the collective narrative (*at least not*

in the way the Greek word proclaims it to be). On an historical

note (remember, I am not a History Geek), the term used for

church (*Ekklesia*) refers to a *public legislative assembly*. It is a

legal term, not a spiritual one. The word *church* comes from

the word *Kirk*, a Celtic word that carries the force and reality

of a European mind. Second, on an institutional level, a *church*

is seen as *either* a body of believers or the building where

they meet, but in the minds of many (*both inside and outside*

the institutional church) it is seen only as the building. Why?

I think it is because the term *Ecclesiology* was coined in the early 1840s to *describe the science of building and designing church buildings.*[131] When the term was coined, it had nothing to do with the people. *Ecclesiology* dealt with the building: how it was designed and how it was built. Over the past 100 years or so, we have tried to make it about people, but I am pretty sure it's not possible. It seems to me that making it about people is not something it was designed to do.

The questions addressed with Ecclesiology tend to support the consumer-based church, the *feed me* church whose people desire to be fed, having a confused belief that if they are fed, they will feed others. The problem is, they demand to eat so much that once fed, they fall asleep only to wake hungry, demanding to eat again. Given that, Ekklesia is not a very good platform to build a theology on – it lacks a personal

---

[131] http://en.wikipedia.org/wiki/Ecclesiology - Accessed 2/22/14

reality, a community reality, a spiritual reality. Let me

introduce the term *Koinonia*[132]and a theology of community

called *Koinology.*

The term *koinonia* appears over 20 times in the collective

narrative, first appearing in the writing entitled *The Acts of the*

Apostles:

> *That day about three thousand took him at his*
> *word, were baptized and were signed up. They*
> *committed themselves to the teaching of the*
> *apostles, the life together, the common meal, and*
> *the prayers.*
>
> *Everyone around was in awe—all those wonders*
> *and signs done through the apostles! And all the*
> *believers lived in a wonderful harmony, holding*
> *everything in common. They sold whatever they*
> *owned and pooled their resources so that each*
> *person's need was met.*

---

[132] http://en.wikipedia.org/wiki/Koininia - Accessed 2/22/14

They followed a daily discipline of worship in the Temple followed by meals at home, every meal a celebration, exuberant and joyful, as they praised God. People in general liked what they saw. Every day their number grew as God added those who were saved.[133]

The wonderful thing about the word *koinonia* is that it is not easily translated into English; no really, that is actually a very cool thing. The passages where the term koinonia is used share vignettes of *Koinology*: everyone sharing with one another, sharing communion, participating in common unity, contributing the needs of others without a selfish thought. They are what I see as a very important reality we should live under when we think of the teachings of the Divine.

A Koinology asks the following questions:

How do we share and live in community?
How does the community of faith view its place in the world?
How should we support those in need?

---

[133] Acts 2:43-47

How can we support the needs of others?

Notice one big difference, with Ecclesiology, we ask "what" (believe) questions, with Koinology we ask "how" (action) questions.

When the Naked Jesus shared communion with us he was showing us how to live in *koinonia*. When he loved others, he was showing us how to live in *koinonia*. When he showed us how to participate with the Divine, he was showing us how to live in *koinonia*. When he showed us how to share what we have with those who have less, he was showing us how to live in *koinonia*; when he showed us to live gather together in unity, he was showing us how to live in *koinonia*. The Naked Jesus is showing us how to center our lives on *koinonia*.

Koinonia has a deep spiritual meaning, not a legal one, set in the following contexts:

Communion
Common unity
Joint participation
A gift jointly contributed
A collection
A contribution

In participation with communion, *koinonia's* spiritual

undertones imply a partnership with the Divine; a partnership

where we share in the life and breath of the Naked Jesus.

Being connected to *koinonia* is a deep spiritual element that

joins us to the Divine and each other. The writer of the letter

to the Philippians says it this way:

> *"If you've gotten anything at all out of following*
> *Christ, if his love has made any difference in your*
> *life, if being in a community of the Spirit means*
> *anything to you, if you have a heart, if you care—*
> *then do me a favor: Agree with each other, love*
> *each other, be deep-spirited friends. Don't push*
> *your way to the front; don't sweet-talk your way*
> *to the top. Put yourself aside, and help others get*
> *ahead. Don't be obsessed with getting your own*

> *advantage. Forget yourselves long enough to lend a helping hand."*[134]

The author of John's first letter adds:

> *"If we claim that we experience a shared life with him and continue to stumble around in the dark, we're obviously lying through our teeth—we're not living what we claim. But if we walk in the light, God himself being the light, we also experience a shared life with one another, as the sacrificed blood of Jesus, God's Son, purges all our sin."*[135]

Koinonia goes beyond the idea of *acceptance* in many congregations. It moves us from simple welcoming and accepting to the reality that we *WANT*: we *want* others connected to us; we *want* to be a community of love, grace and sharing; we *want* to share what we have; and we *want* to participate in life with others and the Divine. *Koinonia* invites

---

[134] Philippians 2:1-4
[135] 1 John 1:6-7

us to live the words of the great '70s theologians, Cheap

Trick,[136] *"I want you to want me."*[137]

When you say your congregation is an *accepting* congregation, what are you saying?

The question I always ask is, *What do you mean by accepting?*

Accepting has lost its power; it has become another marketing slogan of the institutional church that does not imply *wanting*. To move beyond the kitschy slogan, to achieve a *Koinology*, we need to move past *accepting* those the church has historically excluded. *Accepting* people into our communities of faith usually connotes that we have a *tolerance* for who they are, that we *tolerate them*. We need to move beyond

---

[136] http://www.cheaptrick.com/ - Accessed 3/20/14
[137] http://en.wikipedia.org/wiki/I_Want_You_to_Want_Me - Accessed 1/25/14

accepting and tolerating and be a place where the excluded are truly wanted. When we tolerate others, at some level we are saying that their humanity does not matter, but when we want someone, truly want them, we open to inviting them into our lives.

This may be harder than we think because many people have a disconnection between the words *accepted* and *wanted*; they see them as being one in the same. Many believe that to accept *is* to want – but that it not even close to the case. Acceptance is the act of taking, while *wanting* is the act of desire. You can accept a gift without wanting what you received and, if you don't want the gift, you can always return it. Come on, you know what I mean. You accepted that funky shirt from your Aunt Kim last year at Christmas, but there is no way you will wear it because you don't want it.

Caedmon, as it is worthy of being quoted again:

> *"I'm just realizing the irony of "welcoming and*
> *affirming." It is, at face, an act of a privileged*
> *group offering to an oppressed group the*
> *"opportunity" to enter into the privileged world, to*
> *come and be part of the privileged group's culture.*
> *The oppressed members are allowed to maintain*
> *the distinctions of their oppression, but are*
> *otherwise expected to be assimilated into the*
> *privileged culture. This is not justice."*[138]

Where Ecclesiology is a theology of rules, *Koinology* is a

theology of community, an open expression of the self.

Koinology leads to praxis in lifestyle while Ecclesiology settles

on worrying about what your church looks like. Because of its

flexibility, *Koinology* is dynamic, energetic, and connected to

the organic. It is impossible to create a *Systematic Theology*

of Koinology, and that's a good thing. *Koinology* moves us

---

[138] https://www.facebook.com/groups/churchofmisfits/

past privilege and into the realm of connection; moves us past the idea of individuality and into the realm of community where the individual is celebrated.

When I think of the concept of acceptance, I am reminded of the movie *The Greatest Game Ever Played*. In the movie Shia LaBeouf plays *Frances Ouimet*, and amateur golfer who won the 1913 US Open. In one sense, Shia's character is invited into the world of privileged. He is invited into the Golf Courses Country Club for a party to celebrate the US Open. He is standing around, like a duck out of water, when one of the members approaches him and says, "*Young man, you may have been invited, but don't get the idea that you belong here.*" Accepting invites; being *wanted* means you belong.

Koinology far exceeds our understanding of acceptance; it welcomes all, because all are wanted.

According to Wikipedia, acceptance is, "*a person's assent to the reality of a situation, recognizing a process or condition (often a negative or uncomfortable situation) without attempting to change it, protest, or exit.*"[139] Acceptance is tolerating, assenting to the reality of the *negative* or *uncomfortable situation*. We will accept the excluded, but not fully want them, we tolerate them.

I once had a conversation with a Presbyterian (PCUSA) Minister who told me he was OK with "*Those Gays*" coming to his institutional church as long as they did not make it a "*Gay church*" – *accepted but not truly wanted*.

I know a Downtown Church that serves a hot meal to the homeless on Saturday mornings, but directs them to another

---

[139] http://en.wikipedia.org/wiki/Acceptance - Accessed 3/12/14

church in the area for Worship, because "they will feel at home there." – *accepted, but not wanted*.

When we tolerate[140] people, we *allow* them (or grant them the privilege) to enter our sphere but not connect. When we tolerate, we don't make others the core of our faith journey – we put up with them, we endure them, but we never invite them. We think we are doing a good thing by *allowing* them to come into *our* world, but they piss us off so we won't hang with them. If we wanted them, we would have a great desire for them to be part of our Community of Faith, to connect to us, to be welcomed into our community – to be loved for who they are, not what we desire them to be. We would feel relieved, knowing they are in a place with people who love them, want them, and desire only the best for them, no matter the cost to us of the community of faith. Now, I will

---

[140] http://www.thefreedictionary.com/tolerate - Accessed 1/13/14

admit that there are those communities of faith that claim to be accepting, but are actually communities that want others – and this is a good thing.

Koinology teaches us we are in community with each other and the Divine. It is not that we *accept* them into our lives; we actually *want* them in our lives. It has been my understanding that this is not what people mean when they say *we are open and accepting;* sometimes it is, and when it is that is a good thing.

We tolerate people who are LGBTQ, or poor, or have special needs. I found this to be true when several churches I knew wanted to get special permission so they did not have to make their institutional church accessible to those with special needs. A friend, Deb Quilty, says it like this, "*The poor are tolerated and ignored. The working class are accepted, and the wealthy and clergy are celebrated.*" We all desire to be wanted, to be celebrated. *Koinology* is a theology that tells us to celebrate everyone, regardless of who they are or where they come from.

Living a life of *koinonia* means living a life beyond a conditional understanding of a set of qualifiers, usually defined by skin color, gender, culture, gender identity, sexual orientation and others, we go beyond self and into the lives of others. Knowing we are in search of the Naked Jesus and are standing before one another open and naked, labels are hard to justify. People I know want to be wanted for who they are, not for the conditions we place upon them. When we embrace without conditions, we move past acceptance into a wonderful place called *want.* We move from a place where we usurp the responsibility of the Divine to one where we receive people as they are. When the Divine is the only judge, our limited role invites people into our lives without judgment. We don't wash away their identity. We live the revolution, want all, and tell them they are wanted.

Other Books by John Casimir O'Keefe
[All books can be purchased on Amazon.com]

 What will it take for leaders to lead today in the conceptual age? *The Boneyard: Creatives Will Change the Way We Lead in the Church* asks four questions: Where are we now? How did we get here? Where do we need to be? How do we get there? The Boneyard gives six personality traits a conceptual leader needs to move the church forward.

 Who are you including? Many churches today speak of "inclusion," but they define inclusion by who they exclude. *Misfits: Who Are You Including?* is designed to help the church through its exclusion of others into a world of inclusion built on the grace, love and forgiveness of God.

 **The Church Creative:** Creativity is the game changer. If you are willing to rethink, re-imagine, what it means to be a gathering (church) in the 21st century. Creativity can help you move past stagnation, past boring, past lethargy and into a wonderful world where God is expressed in amazing ways. But the question still remains, "How?"

The **Naked** Jesus

[A Journey Out of Christianity and into Christ]

Dr. John Casimir O'Keefe

Ginkworld Publishing
Somewhere on the Planet Earth

The Naked Jesus: [Copyright]

The Naked Jesus; A Journey Out of Christianity and Into Christ.

© 2014 John C. O'Keefe.

Printed in the United States of America

For information on permission to reproduce selections from this book, send an email to: johncasimirokeefe@gmail.com (please include the subject line "*Requesting Permission for use of The Naked Jesus.*")

ISBN-13: 978-1495475832)
ISBN-10: 1495475832

Scripture is quoted from:
Unless otherwise noted, all Scripture is quoted from The Message (MSG), Copyright © 1993, 1994, 1995, 1996, 2000, 2001, 2002 by Eugene H. Peterson.

Chapter Quotes from Brain Quotes (http://www.brainyquote.com/)

Cover Designed by:
   John Casimir O'Keefe and Ginkworld Design.

Cover Pictures are:
   "Homeless Jesus" and "Nude Corpus" sculptures by Timothy P. Schmalz and are used by permission: (http://www.sculpturebytps.com)